GIFTS BRING RIFTS

by Karen Kellock Ph.D.

Manual for Superior Men

A complete theory based on Einstein physics, Political Psychology, Systems Theory and Archetypal Psychiatry.

FORMULA

All success attraction
All disease obstruction
All recovery elimination

You must fast on all three

OBSTRUCTIONS:

People
Habit
Food

GIFTS BRING RIFTS

You're alone but that's the superior state. It's lonely at the top but the only way for success o k. Of all sins the worst is letting people in. To your home, your trust, your confidence, your arms. People are cruel: when you try to escape you see your terrible fate. Don't get involved/evade. How to outsmart the narcissist blocking God's kingdom: get wisdom on the signs and symptoms.

RIFTS

He will now fall into the pit he made for you. His behavior made you go no contact: whew!

CHECKMATE

Going no contact is a lot like declaring checkmate, an ace up your sleeve or winning the lottery.

Tell kids: the most important thing is sovereignty but the most common is INVASION see.

Overcome the narcissist or die. When you finally see the dire options you come to success, aye.

No-contact is the ONLY thing you can control. Do this last thing Madame or grow ugly and old.

Don't get sucked back in! NO-CONTACT is your one--and only--means of controlling demons.

Wives of pastors/churchmen caught with porn end in suicide. Instead of killing him she says byebye.

Once you see how your self-worth's been degraded constantly you LOVE going no contact see.

The most important word is "NO" not "YES" which causes chaos, bedlam, a mess/even death.

MANAGING PEOPLE

It's part of growing up: people DO gossip so you gotta get hep and then learn how to manage it.

See yourself as a precious talented child. Would parents let you date a man that vile?

RIFTS

Going no contact: Though you can't control your thoughts you can control where you walk.

Don't go back--why get messed up? Ahead is a beautiful new vista of real friends and love.

Bad memories are state dependent. How I feel/am fueled inside determines why I cry.

EVERY TIME YOU DON'T GO BACK

For every time you don't go back you're being pushed forward by God who is your heavenly Dad.

I thank you Lord for the pastures, hills and mountains in my view. And everything else too.

Change bad associations and music on the same day and now it's a revolution in your soul ok.

I've definitely landed in a land of milk & honey. Green pastures, rolling hills and nice people see.

What a relief not having to get their approval anymore, or running things thru them like a filter.

As I see the view I thank God for every minute cuz I know He values gratitude: it's what I do.

No matter where it occurs in the world, at the end of civilizations Satanic cults take over.

It's part of growing up: people DO gossip so you gotta get hep and then learn how to manage it.

"She goes after what she wants" but women should never chase men: it's not the way it was.

Let your work stand on its own. You can retire now, stop trying cuz you've done it all you know.

RIFTS

You don't need that guy, it's a mirage you thinking you do. Get into the destiny God has for YOU.

The answer to heartbreak is JUST get into your own thing. Honest darling, that's everything.

You gotta be whole before a real relationship anyway. It's a trip of glory: you don't need anybody.

Just when you get to that point God'll bring in your mate. Be ready to take this option ok.

EXPLORE YOUR TINY CORNER

Get into your tiny corner of the universe and I guarantee you won't think of that curse.

He's disregulated. He can't control is raging impulses nor does he intend or think he needs to.

God sent you a mirage to test you. Would you again get hoovered into a rabbit hole coocoo?

He gave so little you're addicted to the possibility. Don't you want a loving relationship honey?

Stay in your tiny corner of the universe and thank God for it. Never covet for God won't bless it.

He gave so little you filled it in with fantasy and became addicted to that, what a story!

Avoid flashy charismatic for he discards after he gets it and there's new supply when he exits.

The herd sees aging as wearing out of parts but superior men see it as wholeness, an exemplar.

I am never not sitting at a table facing my PC and the view. All I say is whata life, Lord Thank You.

INTIMIDATION

INTIMIDATION

LOW POINTS ON THE PATH
HILLS AND VALLEYS

There are very dark phases on the Hero's Path: like the season of treason which is hellish and bad.

The higher your walls and disgust the earlier you react to a mess {inferring you're less} and you reject.

After suffering betrayal trauma once you run away at the slightest indication it'll happen twice.

She's a vicious slanderer and mistress of half-truths blown up to destroy you for good dude.

He knows what he's doing, why he's doing it but pleads ignorance. Expect this from a narcissist.

You're no one's OPTION. It's severe degradation like other comparisons cuz you're the queen man.

The heartbreaking damage a narcissist can do means going no-contact is the only way to heal.

Social anxiety controls behavior making us inferior rather than heroes changing a sick culture.

YOU WILL NOT BE CONDEMNED

God said repentant shall not be condemned. No matter WHAT we did the image is mended.

The saints have a stinging conscience while the ordinary guy couldn't care less.

INTIMIDATION

When finally mature they were heroic/valiant see, free of colossal self-destructive stupidity.

Don't ever tell him why and don't swear, cuss or get back. You're a queen so just walk away fast.

Let his aesthetic knowledge take over cuz he knows what/why he's doing it, it's subconscious.

GOD WANTS YOU TO BE HAPPY

Just see him as one you'll never allow to [get a chance to] hurt you again, then you're done.

To the clear one word stands for **WORLDS**. One word or gesture is enough to show what he is girl.

They are ever excited by new supply, the chase, a new partner in any case. Easily bored = narcissist.

Build character by never checking spam folder. Never forget why you put him there/it's over.

Smart well-spoken men at twenty are the elders, not men in their sixties still chasing ____.

The higher your walls the higher your level of disgust and that's the best word to describe it sis.

What he does he does intentionally. It's more important to show off than protect feelings/no empathy.

SAD EFFECTS OF NARCISSISTIC ABUSE

The effects of narcissistic abuse can go on for decades or death. Find a stable man/enjoy life instead.

You learn to expect it from a man so when it happens it's an instant reaction and a ban, amen?

INTIMIDATION

For the temporary thrill of showing off to the guys he lost a queen cuz it's him she despises.

The higher your walls the higher your disgust. You gotta get your disgust back: pray for this.

A true lady has had enough of [putting up with] perverted male society showing off to itself.

We've had enough of boomer men hurting women. That women-hate trend is dangerous and mean.

FOG OF MENTAL ILLNESS TIL MATURE

She was in a fog of mental illness for decades but then with maturity rose to a station of highness.

Yes you were immature but God knew what you were before you were even born, so persevere.

See yourself as a tender and talented child with a mother and father who are actively involved.

In trying to make her jealous you lost her for good Mr. Ridiculous but that's how you are I guess.

LURKING AND SPYING

Checking spam is giving the devil an opportunity to hook you in and that's too big a gamble hon'.

Build character by never going back. In modern age it's easy to lurk but that keeps you a sad sack.

Every time she lurks and spies her self-esteem leaks. You gotta forget this guy then speak.

Call me or someone to report to. If you slip and lurk you leak self-worth and could see worse too.

INTIMIDATION

If you love yourself you won't go back or lurk. He didn't even deserve a conversation the jerk.

See lurking/spying as bad as parking in front of his house. The self-esteem leak is even worse.

As they see our SMV going down they think nothing of asking ridiculous favors nor do they care.

FORGETTING THE DARK VALLEYS

He was just an illusion, a bridge of dust but a good lesson. Stay home and stop your chasin'.

Try to forget the downpoints as just part of the path. Even the black sheep/fallen hero is part of it.

He knew what you would do before you did it and even tho' you have free choice He still knew it.

It's like all past actors are sitting in your living room ragging on you. Clear the brain/enjoy the view.

They hated the devil in you but after repentance you kinda remember all this and it smarts too.

Who were they hating, hitting, smearing? Ruining the rep of, trouble causing? Heartbreaking.

If war refugees swilled in specific details they'd never heal. Put it all in a bag marked "raw deal".

RAW DEAL PHASE

The raw deal phase was your season of treason, those low points on your path which everyone has.

All the crap you went thru was preknown by God too. It made you who you are, a seer and muse.

INTIMIDATION

You can't grow without courage to be disliked because systems reverberate with growth, aye.

CHEATING AND BOUNDARIES

Relationships: if you don't create the design and set the template you'll get what they give you ok.

If you don't define boundaries right off it's a lot harder to deal with and things can get rough.

What is cheating to you: pornography, looking at other women or youth comparisons? Review.

What ruffles your feathers: coming without calling first, bringing friends, calling you at work?

You get so sharp that ONE WORD indicates WORLDS and you know everything about him girl.

Cheating is a hot topic and makes my gut turn to think about it but you learn to walk away quick.

Gut aches from fickle fakes was recurrent through life and it's a terrifying feeling--but God saved.

The ONLY opinion about which constitutes cheating is yours and yours alone. Ignore all else son.

You get advice from those with loose and permissive thinking on cheating: run away sweetie.

All I know is I can't take it and around you I get stomach aches. My body tells me what cheating is.

DEFINE IT OR ACCEPT THE RESULTS

Cheating: a violation of understanding to the terms of the relationship. Now, did you ever define it?

INTIMIDATION

Someone stepped outa line and broke a trust of connection. Define it and then connect again.

Is talking to an ex cheating, is microcheating [flirting] a gut-wrenching trigger for a drinking spree?

Are office flirtations cheating, or hanging around/getting a little too close to someone socially?

What about stepping over the boundaries to test whether you're still desirable to groupies?

FROM MID AGED LECHER TO AN ELDER

He hasn't grown up yet, he's still a middle-aged lecher not a kindly elder gentleman so GTH man.

Don't ever tell him why you left cuz he'll attack you for it. Just be a cat: get away & catapult up.

If you don't set up ground rules at the beginning then you get what you get and have to deal with it.

If you don't have the guts to say what you need in a relationship here comes abuse: who needs it.

Some people see kissing as cheating, others see full-on sexual intercourse as the thing see.

A monogamist is focused, intentional and wants a quality investment: the best of all he's got.

People cheat less for sex than a life force, a vibrancy, a feeling alive again. Promising youth: Satan.

Don't minimize jealousy. We're still animals and territorial: open marriages have issues like all.

Emotional cheating: Everything they should come to you about they go to someone else see.

INTIMIDATION

An intrusive ex who's always around injecting herself into the mind of your beloved husband.

There's an intrusive ex who's always there cuz the partner lacks the boundaries to protect the core.

Another person comes in and now you need a discussion on rules of intimacy or you're gone.

Cheating is a breach indicating one went beyond boundaries established at the beginning.

You're not a flake for making a decision on what you can and cannot take and then walking hell away.

BLOOD IN THE WATER

If weak, shattered and exposed after a breakup you'll be invaded by dark clowns and other parasites.

Here he cheats on you then takes the highroad about it, as if you're mentally ill to even bring it up.

Here he cheats then dominates your mind demanding you feel and see it his way: FLY AWAY.

It's like putting a rattlesnake in your cage. Any minute you can be shocked, terrified, attacked ok.

I already had to train one husband how to treat me, I don't wanna go thru that again see.

I got my pretty face on, the whole bit. Got dandy duds and a gig cuz I planned every inch of it.

Compare me with younger women to trigger insecurity and I'm gone cuz I'm not a masochist see.

It's perverted male culture or independence and a gentleman like you were years before sir.

INTIMIDATION

Like moths to a flame all those things they're sayin' are null/void/erased cuz God's your Champion.

Gossip goes empty, shot to hell and never existed because it's not of God and they're just twisted.

DARK DUNGEON OF COMPARISONS

I'd never go back to that dark dungeon of being with a man comparing me to younger women.

Like throwing me into competition, or somehow flaunting them to make me alert/conform.

An older woman doesn't have time for common head games so byebye creep, so long lame.

The mere fact he'd even do that shows he's cruel about something you have no control over too.

It's the cornucopia of joyous and abundant right-brain living vs. the dark dungeon of comparisons.

Due to compulsion to push the envelope it was you who finally broke the soul tie, thank you dope.

Your entire past collapses thru fasting or relocating. In an instant it's a bad dream you're forgetting.

DON'T LET EM INTO YOUR HOME

Don't let em into your home. Here's where you gotta get a thick skin and really build assertion.

Ye is the perversion of the new age view that all men are good with something to contribute.

It's like the all-forgiving religious lady who creates convicts cuz they're never corrected.

INTIMIDATION

To a creative artist nothing hurts so much as conformity and trashing the creative impulse.

CONTROL MIND OR GET SICK

There are some so hypersensitive that to not control their mind creates physical illness.

Mind is a battlefield and Satan loves to bring up the past for a fear and adrenalin blast.

I had no control. Over and over I'd go down the same rabbit hole angry/remorseful/fearful.

Hate is a poison and in the end you only poison yourself. D. Bundestag, Holocaust survivor.

NAZI SIBLINGS AND SYMPTOMS

If not in control of your own behavior something else is and it's sadly inferior.

Unplug from old systems, close the door. Life's too short/you wanna SOAR not be bored.

In Nazi Germany the idea was to break down individuality and build the collective spirit.

The most sadistic Nazi camp guards were women. Sister abuse feels like that, a dark cavern.

They call us criminals, pickpockets, pimps, drug dealers, slavers and hack journalists.

We were all jealous of the girls with blond hair and blue eyes, that's the influence of Nazis.

Said before an execution: "If someone doesn't shoot him dead Hitler will lead us into ruin."

Don't complain, don't explain. Silence is golden cuz it fits every crevice and is always perfect ok.

INTIMIDATION

There are some so hypersensitive that to not control their mind creates physical illness.

Those who can't make the grade are ritually humiliated. This happens in families, sororities, cities.

When the proud see no way out they will glorify their downfall. Playing victim is their last call.

Ye is no different than the cop-defunding murderer-releasing culture we're suffering now sir.

New Age doesn't see good or bad, it's all good in fact--save those drawing lines against cads.

We are seeing the results of lawlessness: a land without judgement/justice and it's hellish.

JUNKARDS: PEOPLE AND STUFF

I don't hold onto stuff cuz it holds me back. I've given away tons for CLARITY/success in fact.

Don't be a materialist married to your stuff. You'll never touch it again yet you hang on: yuk!

Move on! Disencumber yourself, enjoy the exhilaration of clarity: be the RICH magic elf.

Don't pay for storage just give it all way. Man you need clarity, these things are anchors of doom ok?

CULMINATION AND COMPLETION

Gotta cut back on my orange juice drinking. I love it as heavenly but acid at night is overwhelming.

Take a toke, put on chillout. Wait for the bubble to come up and then write the pearl/quip.

INTIMIDATION

An artist will reflect his sickness. Be careful who's the cover artist/he could be a haunted house sis.

It saves so much time only listening to your own mind. No more outer input, just going inside.

Sunday is the day to review your work. Take it in, stand way back and admire a masterpiece first.

I got my duds and my face on, I'm ready to speak. I've overcome all but they're still up a creek.

If you came from a crazy blue state you'll be crazy for awhile when you get here, just persevere.

As America crumbles Biden's handing out metals, seeking approval of movie stars now.

People with most power defend people with the least power in order to crush you sucker.

The very people worrying over our "democracy" are the ones disrupting our democracy constantly.

We'll dry your tears [from PTSD after relocating] but please don't bring your perverse politix here.

GIFTS STOLEN

BRUTAL, CALLOUS AGEISM
WHEN VIEWED AS A CATEGORY
EFFECTS OF AGEISM
WORD CURSES
JEALOUSY: BYE BYE
THE DEVIL IS THE ACCUSER
QUEENS: THEY BLAME YOU
HOW THE QUEEN HEALS
UNDERSTAND HIM BUT LEAVE HIM
WE ALWAYS TAKE THE BLAME
YOU HUNG AROUND FOR THE PARTY
ATTRACTED TO TRAUMA BUTTERFLIES
WHAT LIES DID I BUY?
NOT A LITTLE GIRL, MEEK AND HUMBLE
THEY NEED INVO ONLY YOU CAN GIVE
BROKEN QUEENS CHOOSE SEX ATTRACTION
DISCERNMENT: HE ISN'T FOR YOU
YOUR "TYPE" IS A FIGMENT OF FLESH
WOMEN MUST INSPIRE MEN
FORGIVE BUT DON'T FORGET
YOUR HIGHER AND LOWER SELF
STUCK IN WOUNDED REALITY

GIFTS STOLEN

I bought what a bully said about me and degraded to that degree for a quarter of a century.

The solution to the cruel undertow against women is the queen archetype of having overcome.

I know how much it hurt but God promises a great future and also a mate who is healthy/safe.

BRUTAL, CALLOUS AGEISM

A real man would do anything before asking a woman for money but gigolos are accepted honey.

The mean ageist-youthist mentality is: you're inferior cuz you've been on earth a little longer.

In traditional cultures the aged are given the first seat in the senate and control of family till the end.

Deeper values long distilled like fine wine can only come from sagacious elders yet we're maligned.

Shit shots on age: she's jealous of your house so in a natural homeostasis puts you in your place.

Ageism takes over in callous, shallow generations. Lift up your voice like a trumpet, tell all about em.

While he body recedes the brain expands as temporal lobes reveal eternity: that's elder sagacity.

WHEN VIEWED AS A CATEGORY

GIFTS STOLEN

To be suddenly viewed as a category not a person is hell on earth if you are wise/self-approving.

To be suddenly viewed as a category not a person is hell on earth if you are wise/self-approving.

Consigned to a category due to age? No, this is the height of rudeness and destroying a sage.

I had a peculiar adeptitude [knack] but it didn't come out till late--post-feuds and being a sad sack.

EFFECTS OF AGEISM

Her mom suffered rejection, gave up to please herself feeling entitled, a 2 year old wanting her way.

Never force your work because when it's time it'll all come out like a tsunami until it is done.

Ageism says in effect: it doesn't matter what you've done you're an old bag and they're young.

Ageism: it doesn't matter that SHE'S old, that's not the game. She can put you down just the same

An older woman knows how it feels so she insults you with it--you end up feeling like an old twit.

It's easier to isolate as an older queen, the endless battle with the undertow is so mean.

Femi-Nazis know how it feels very well so of course they use it as a weapon against younger victims.

You won't get the perks of an older woman if from the undertow in society you're driven down.

Their toxic influence happens by the mere contact. It's contact-conquest so get behind a fence.

GIFTS STOLEN

WORD CURSES

Subtle "word curses" make you rethink your own worth. They stay with you as black clouds emerge

They'll see your fecundity which is undeniable see, then you will publicly sprout like a watered tree.

After decades on mute they'll now see: your brilliant light will no longer be hidden God said to me.

Your own sister took an inconsequential error and blew it up to cover earth in her lifelong slander.

You were discarded, you were betrayed by your own family, you lost everything to a soul tie.

That's how the inferior fight their wars: through vicious cowardly gossip to harden people's fears.

JEALOUSY: BYE BYE

The most successful president of the modern age is being trashed by Fox and other traitors.

The narcissists will move you outa the way. With the slightest bit of jealousy it's bye bye baby.

Not only is this narcissistic trauma painful it has long term physical consequences too.

Autoimmune conditions, cancer and countless other illnesses erupt in these mal-adaptations.

How dangerous it is to let someone have access to YOU and your LIFE. Why make this sacrifice?

After years of taking this situation we ghost them now and we send NO letters of explanation.

GIFTS STOLEN

When hitting a problem glitch is it something you should break through or definitely eschew?

Never let narcissist know how much you know about him. Just get on with your happy life, amen.

"All Uphill Now" movie refers to leaving desert/the valley of low self-esteem and adapting to mean.

The extent to which a person will go to break you would blow your mind grasping the full meaning.

The power of ACCUSATION is the center of the demonic. The blame game creates lunatics.

They know they're wrong but reverse situation to accuse you--get it straight, it's classic narcissism.

After reversing the situation to blame you now they will ghost you and I guarantee this to be true.

THE DEVIL IS THE ACCUSER

They accuse you--making a big deal--then pull away so you can marinate in confusion awhile.

The accusation is so beneath you it brings desperate attempts to correct it, but they ghost you.

Sometimes you gotta love them at their level, which is a far distance if you're a survivor at all.

You gotta know when to walk away. Is it the right time now, today? Cuz he will never change ok.

Because narcissism is a disorder: they see/love you as an extension then soon discard in that order.

Narcissism is about REVERSALS without conscience or the slightest tinge of empathy for innocents.

GIFTS STOLEN

The curse is your desperate tries to prove innocence when they're gone and couldn't care less.

They don't want you getting closure/addressing the issue, just to marinate in the confusion Sue.

In the confusion you're devaluing yourself because you're questioning yourself, it's synonymous.

When the narcissist reverses on you, you try to get him back. No, you should walk away in fact.

QUEENS: THEY BLAME YOU

They blame you, then ghost you and later pop back up. This is hoovering but you can make it stop.

A queen never lets divorce define her, she always repairs her soul and to the throne she returns.

A queen can't escape the blows hurled at women but still standing, she returns to her role then.

Everything you went thru like smear campaigns didn't break you and proved you still stand too.

A queen is calm, confident, present but trauma robs lesser females who get nervous, jittery, wretched.

Her confidence shines but with trauma this is all drained out: lackluster, exhausted, blocked.

She's afraid to take action cuz her soul is broken. She's become pessimistic, no longer hopeful.

A queen is present: not drawn into negative past, conversation/thoughts don't reflect the mess.

HOW THE QUEEN HEALS

GIFTS STOLEN

Nor is she way in the future worrying over what may happen. She plans but stays present.

She observes the background of the one who hurt her: the brokenness of the man who broke her.

The only way a man could hurt a woman is to be severely damaged himself, for one reason.

A conscious man is always seeking to avoid hurting women. So when one does, he is vermin.

A healthy man sees doing damage to his wife is doing damage to himself--he breaks his own rib.

UNDERSTAND HIM BUT LEAVE HIM

Understanding is no excuse to stay in a toxic system but it will enable the great healer: forgiveness.

They did it due to immaturity [couldn't see the whole], hormones and collective insanity see.

A man's soul is broken who breaks the soul of a woman. Groups exchange notes on how it's done.

A generation of men galvanize to hurt a generation of women, gossipping in detail about em.

Even when she's wrong a real man leaves her to her folly but won't participate in treachery.

Her new understanding shifts her from victim status into compassion for the victimizing victim.

Without understanding it becomes a loop in which we're stuck: Why did they do this to me, why...

WE ALWAYS TAKE THE BLAME

GIFTS STOLEN

Toxic mind says "you deserved it, you're inferior" when in reality broken people break others.

The concept of broken people breaking others empowers/ignites forgiveness, the total answer.

Queens easily forgive and stay present. Unforgiveness locks us in the past, it's all we think about.

You forgive and move on. You don't allow unforgiveness to get you stuck with ghosts long gone.

It had nothing to do with you. You just had a broken person in your life who did what they do.

YOU HUNG AROUND FOR THE PARTY

You hung around for the party tho' it wasn't thrown in your honor--you caused your own trauma.

The narc traumatizes you, claims victimhood when you're through and the breakup's your fault too.

She's now trapped in the cycle of believing she needs to get better to be loved, respected, honored.

It's not her fault he can't see her or value her. But it feels like it is in this cycle so circular.

Question: why was she so vulnerable, WHY did she let him into her life when he's filled with strife?

What was deficient in the queen to allow her toleration of that jester let alone having an affair?

Instead blaming a clown in a crown, search your own deficiencies being so vulnerable to him.

She avoids healthy/safe men due to a previous trauma uncorrected and is led to the cliff, rejected.

GIFTS STOLEN

ATTRACTED TO TRAUMA BUTTERFLIES

She's attracted to a trauma based on butterflies in her gut—an adrenalin rush feeling like love.

Attracted to adrenalin a safe guy's not given a chance cuz he doesn't do the dysfunction dance.

So if first we understand him, then we ask whats wrong with us to be with such a man: question.

Tho' deficiencies aren't obvious to her they are to predators saying exactly what she wants to hear.

They know exactly what profile they need to present and this poor war-torn victim eats it up.

WHAT LIES DID I BUY?

For healing you ask "what lies did I internalize?" They all changed your self-estimation by this guy.

Change your self-estimation and he can mark your price down. Liars with smiles wants this known.

Self-interrogation speeds the process of healing. Clay covered in silver is unpeeling and revealing.

He who hates disguises it with his lips while storing up deceit in his heart. Do not trust him/depart.

He may disguise how he feels while seven abominations are in his heart. Don't let him in/don't start.

Tho' he hides it malevolence is openly revealed to the assembly—shouted from the rooftops honey.

Backstabbers smile in your face then drop certain buzz words that kill the spirit, making you joyless.

GIFTS STOLEN

Life was a puzzle I had to solve just to survive. A cat in a roomful of rocking chairs was my life.

She was always deflated as he took the wind out of her sails/rained on her parade--till she escaped.

NOT A LITTLE GIRL, MEEK AND HUMBLE

You can't be a little girl again but meek and humble coming as a child to God/your only Friend.

In your 70's you're meek and humble as a child, Ghandi archetype, a fastarian resisting the hype.

You were consigned to a Magdalene asylum way out in desert wilderness never to be seen again.

You were convicted by gossip without judge or jury only because they hated women see.

If they hate women to begin with they'll believe what they want to blowing it up to everyone too.

Don't believe what you see, mock the fancy disguise of treachery. Trust no man/it's not just hes.

THEY NEED INVO ONLY YOU CAN GIVE

You're giving it all you can/doing your best shot at the end, your last hurrah so they can mend.

Now let the adrenalin flow because it's about your art form and success, how God will bless.

Success can also bring panic, like an alcoholic who drinks at it. Ask God of this/do your duty darnit.

They need info only you can give. You've been thru things quite horrible so tell em how to live.

GIFTS STOLEN

You can't know if a man gets another chance if you're high on desperation and lessened by that.

Now draft your own constitution of how you will be treated--not like the world does, defeated.

Learning from experience [putdowns and ruination] is much harder than learning from instruction.

Letting go of what was never meant to be evokes "toxic nostalgia" but that will pass I promise ya.

When accepting it was never meant to be she returns her focus to things of home and destiny.

In her life of big hurts she never realized being in touch with herself was the most important sir.

Her "type" refers to sexual attraction but that won't be what gives her the biggest life satisfactions.

BROKEN QUEENS CHOOSE SEX ATTRACTION

The broken queen chooses sex attraction while having nothing in common spiritually/mentally son.

Not only is man omnivorous, he's oligophagous: able to exist on fewest varieties of foods around us.

There's a strain of women-hate and if you don't get a nice mate you could get real hurt ok.

Let him be someone else's problem now. You've had it with this merry go round/hell you've known.

The good heart always wants to see the best in people but overlooks things that are clearly evil.

The good heart created pre-convicts by her All is Good attitude and looking the other way too.

GIFTS STOLEN

At some point we gotta grow up emotionally and see the world as it is, NOT what we wish it to be.

Despite his good looks/hitting all the marks, if not the right energy that's God saying RUN see.

They pass all the tests but if not the GUT test, that's God saying I Do Not Approve, so resist.

It was a nightmare living in the liberal state of California but in flyover country I'm free/full privacy.

If you don't pick up the right spirit on a person, run. If only I'd listened to myself way back then.

He passed the eye test, he hit all the marks but I didn't feel right about him in my spirit/no sparks.

DISCERNMENT: HE ISN'T FOR YOU

The church calls it discernment: they are not meant for you if you don't feel good in your SPIRIT.

I felt pure hate coming from him. Was it for me or all women? I don't know I just wanted to run.

To recapitulate for God's great: God is saying "this is not for you" if you feel it in your spirit ok.

Too many of us ignore the fact a spirit doesn't agree with ours, maybe cuz they're millionaires.

The black sheep may feel unhappy with his whole family system--feeling homesick when with them.

That relationship is not ordained by God. It is easy to get involved but honey it's hell to get out of.

What if she's attracted to bad boys? A little edgy, unpredictable, scary--and she marries?

GIFTS STOLEN

The wise ones learn there's gonna be more to life than sexual attraction and choosing your "type".

Samson kept going after his "type" who kept betraying him and ended up destroying him.

Wise women know a man who is her "type" may not be her "kind". That's values, goals, plans.

Wise women know to make long term decisions not based on superficial temporary situations.

A man who is her type rarely makes a good husband which is chosen from the soul and spirit.

YOUR "TYPE" IS A FIGMENT OF FLESH

Your type is just a figment of your flesh, a product of your carnality and hypnotized worldliness.

Type is what moves you but a husband is far deeper than that, he co-creates your future too.

Wasting youth on useless things has a severe price. You had no models, just worldly waste & strife.

I need a man who shows the same approach to life. The wise ones learn that and they thrive.

You've been into this hot girl stuff for fifteen years and it's getting old. Let this all go, find the gold.

So he's your type but he blows his nose in his shirt and won't pick up his socks/shirts, a real jerk.

Cute and pretty won't pay bills but most importantly: it doesn't last but a couple of weekends see.

Intelligence is beautiful for life. Go beyond your physical enhancements which don't last, aye.

GIFTS STOLEN

Cute & pretty don't pay bills or hang around long. You need brains and vision for the future hon'.

When you are a woman who's mastered her own mind with a clear vision you bow to NO one.

The wise ones understand this. They work on their brains, business, vision and they the boss.

The point is never to be in a position where you must sleep with someone to pay the rent hon'.

The question: will you learn these vital truths thru safe instruction or harsh life experiences?

Chivalry battles against all evildoers, defends all women, is true in friendship, faithful in love.

WOMEN MUST INSPIRE MEN

Women inspire men to do masterpieces but then obstruct them from carrying them out.

Everyone's life has hills and valleys but you overcame it all--that's the whole point, you're whole.

Everyone has hills and valleys and those were yours. Other than that, try to forget those years.

You can't know if a man gets another chance if you're high on desperation and lessened by that.

You can give him another chance if he doesn't have a history of the same behavior, alas.

If a brother wrongs you he will ask forgiveness then give you space--not ever pressuring you ok.

Love does not pressure. If you tell me to shove it under the rug and forget it that's not right either.

GIFTS STOLEN

You've never obligated to give anyone space back in your life if they used it to hurt you, aye.

Many women waste their entire lives on someone who should have never gotten a conversation.

If a man can't own what he did without excuses--I hurt you, I'm sorry--he doesn't get back in too.

People say you're wrong for not allowing a hurtful person back in after forgiving him--ignore em.

FORGIVE BUT DON'T FORGET

Forgiving and forgetting are two separate things. Forgive but never have to see em again see.

If after hurting you he's not emotionally accommodating ["stop your questions"] that's also a bad sign.

You wanna see if his words match his actions--those will be shown before any words are spoken.

A mother transmits feminine divine energy to her daughter who then develops the same see.

A healthy mind sees oneself as worthy of love and respect but a sick mind self-destructs.

Feminine energy is compassionate/forgiving/creative. If daughter's denied this she loses spirit.

Who is available when mom isn't? The higher self is always there so kindly instruct her in this.

One may find his higher self while in jail or after a season of treason where friendships failed.

YOUR HIGHER AND LOWER SELF

Your lower self: appetites, angers, doubts, addictive tendencies. Higher self: perfect and free.

GIFTS STOLEN

How the lower self solves it: something bad happens and you fall into your bag of crutches.

Don't be obsessed with valleys in the past. Be like a war victim: you wanna forget it all and fast.

The family bully hounded you to near death. Tho' exhausted you will revive with no-contact.

If denied love from mom she's disconnected from the female energy within-- it's a dark canyon.

STUCK IN WOUNDED REALITY

Now she's stuck in the wounded reality of the inner child. Abandonment wounds take over, aye.

The child takes the blame for abandonment and then the inner critic takes over: I'm a bagashit.

The human biocomputer gets screwed up seeking approval from a faulty, dualistic personality.

Those who gravitate to this information tend to be wounded healers, persecuted artists, empaths.

Alcoholic mothers are fueled by addiction which is fueled by abandonment-- inescapable pain.

We come into world and snap into mom's grid, aligning with her energy and karma it is said.

Be an exemplar to the youth, that's how you handle it. Not be their pal by degrading like a twit.

Preface
GIFTS BRING RIFTS

PAINFUL RECOGNITIONS
SEASON OF TREASON
PUSH AWAY THE IMPOSERS/SHAMERS
SHAME WORK IS CRUCIAL
JEALOUSY IMPUTES SHAME
GROUP SHAME TYRANNY
SHAMEE IS SORRY FOR EXISTING
SHAME IMPUTATION TO MAINTAIN STATION
SHAME FOR HOMEOSTASIS
TAMING OF THE INSTINCTS
PROPLE PROJECT THEIR CRAP
FRANTIC SEARCH FOR PEACE
SHE'S GUILTY FOR WHAT HE'S THINKING
CRUTCHES BRING MORE ATTACKS
EMPATH HYPERSENSITIVE/BOUNDARIES
MONEY SOLVES ALL THINGS
ONLY INDEPENDENCE IS FREEDOM
HATED FOR BEING DIFFERENT
STOP ANCHORING BACKWARD
RIGID HIERARCHIES ARE HELL SEE
IMMEDIATE PUNISHMENTS FOR DISSIDENCE
RECAP: SHAMERS ARE DOUBLESPEAK

Preface
GIFTS BRING RIFTS

Allowed to develop on our own accord we'd be fine but then someone invasive comes along.

Boundaries, boundaries, boundaries is the issue. Need a protective cocoon that's just you.

The only time I was happy was in solitude. I was being put thru a ringer by that girl/dude.

It was horrible before I knew. An open book, naive but true, unprotected from the coocoo.

She's molested by some creep and her life changes forever as it permeates all other areas.

Cut the dross so that now God's creative spirit can come thru fresh, unadulterated and new.

In making gold we repent of a crutch then separate out these elements: like sorting socks.

Don't argue about your constitutional right to privacy, just shut the dam door. Wake up girl.

After her imposition/season of treason a black cloud came over me: I went decades on empty.

PAINFUL RECOGNITIONS

Welcome to the club when you find out your spouse, mom, sister, aunt and best friend told all.

Put all memory in a bag, throw it out and don't go back. All kinds of things happen cuz it's Satan.

Preface: GIFTS BRING RIFTS

I was an aging baby and it was all about boundaries. The people I let in showed total stupidity.

They call your aversion to evil anti-social because they're evil too: it's a form of denial.

Gifts bring rifts: whether beauty or intellect on the ego of other women there's a BIG effect.

Just being different cast you in bad light then they pasted on despicable details of your blight.

SEASON OF TREASON

Get thru the season of treason/false accusation. You'll be standing there strong from the lesson.

For when you have negative core beliefs about yourself it acts as a program or roadmap to hell.

The world's gatekeepers wanna bring you down but God laughs in derision at these arrogant clowns.

I felt whole and bright but would splinter at their slights. That's not wellness or being a knight.

To still love myself despite what others see when they look at me: this is healthy minded and free.

The frail psych folds at ridicule. It breaks into pieces in fretful, pitiful denials kissing up to fools.

PUSH AWAY THE IMPOSERS/SHAMERS

Who are you? Perfectly imperfect and saved by grace. Undeserved I might add but holy in any case.

Don't cling or push but be neutral. That means pushing things away that wanna cling like a barnacle.

Preface: GIFTS BRING RIFTS

We're hard enough on ourselves, we don't need the world's attacks with its made-up insults.

Shame is covering up who you are and the truth you're meant to advance on this earth as a star.

With negative self-talk always remind yourself to call out toxic shame: something you are NOT.

The reborn psych has space thru the healing process to exist, to be and to call out all projections.

Heal and decide: that's me, that's not me. I've a right to exist and you're wrong about that see.

The whole can tolerate your existence which is separate from there's. The low can't do this in fear.

We gotta refuse and give back the negative projections of others. That's the recap of what follows.

SHAME WORK IS CRUCIAL

There is "shame work" where she gives it back to the perpetrator, to the one laying it on her.

Shame work is major in therapy: putting it on ya is how they keep you down and controlled honey.

I give this shame back with a right to exist as I am not as he/she expects me to be: that's the gist.

For if you take on the projections of others it will dim you light/turn a rainbow to a bad night.

By reacting to negative emotions which they place upon you it confirms their conflicts too.

You now hold the shame of the whole world since you didn't give it back or refuse to receive it.

Preface: GIFTS BRING RIFTS

I soaked in the shame others put upon me like a sponge. It created havoc, distrust and no change.

Honoring self and analyzing what's coming in [causing you to feel down and less-than] stops it.

Healthy shame is wholesome but toxic shame is when you're taking it in from someone else ok.

The shame giver wants you to react with those feelings so you become a carrier of the shame see.

The more shame you accept determines the more you get: the default setting is harmful effect.

Learned helplessness sets in, defeated until you can't move on, debased to an ineffectual slob.

JEALOUSY IMPUTES SHAME

With imputed shame you let yourself go. You're in denial and look pasty, the opposite to glow.

No one can make you feel this way, you've accepted the shame but have the ability to say no ok.

Instead of feeling a red blush come over you, STOP right here and push it back to the giver to chew.

It's a ploy, a tactic and it's automatic to maintain status but seeing the setup acts as a backstop.

Similarly, if you feel misjudged it's an offense and you move away not drink, snort or stuff ok.

Assuming bad things about you is an offense. You don't stuff/use at it, you return it to the dense.

The imputed shame from sister Jane was so toxic I walked around in a fog, unable to explain.

Preface: GIFTS BRING RIFTS

It's a skill sorting out what impacts and what doesn't, of guarding heart from disillusionment.

GROUP SHAME TYRANNY

When a group comes against you shame intensifies. Learn how one man is a majority/group lies.

Withdraw, isolate, fast, pray and read the psalms how the kings collude together on a matter.

They lay crap on you/make sure the world agrees too. Detach, fast knowing Psalm's words are true.

Personal development and boundaries helps delineate what's in your lane vs. someone elses ok.

What you own/what you don't. What pertains vs. manipulative shame. When to go home/stay.

How to stand up straight in your own lane and rebound when your hit by imputed shame again.

No matter how prepared your boundaries are, you might again accept shame that's not yours.

You may even think you're doing a favor by accepting shame but it's to your detriment ok.

Individuation is being a whole person and stepping back from thoughts and feelings pasted on.

So much trouble comes from shame pasted on by someone who's mad, jealous or feels entitled.

SHAMEE IS SORRY FOR EXISTING

The immature feel they owe an apology for existing or deny themselves the right to speaking.

Preface: GIFTS BRING RIFTS

By accepting their shame the light goes from your eyes and all energy drains as only ugly remains.

Stop, take note of shame being put upon you. Say: this isn't mine, I don't receive it and he's coocoo.

I now return the shame to the original source so I walk freely, the way I was before this war.

Walk in your authentic truth/ability to maintain wholeness facing attacks from Satan's crew.

Your sister imputes shame in your 20s and you release the fog in your 60s: that's too long honey.

Whole, you will face splintering obstructions, like walking into a buzzsaw. Prepare, that's all.

Don't feel shame for what you can't do for them at their request. Dare to deny demanders at least.

Practice this today: No matter what they say hit the ball back to where it belongs then step away.

SHAME IMPUTATION TO MAINTAIN STATION

Much shame-imputation comes from jealousy or maintaining a station. It's homeostasis son.

Shame was a problem. An aching sense of self-disgust always hanging around yet unknown.

Shame: someone else wanted to hold me down or who's ego was shaken by talents coming out.

By holding shame I'm resolving something for them. It's despicable to sacrifice self this way, amen.

By accepting shame the psychotic child feels she's saving the mother from crazy or suicide.

41

Preface: GIFTS BRING RIFTS

SHAME FOR HOMEOSTASIS

Accepting shame for homeostasis [holding the system together, the status quo] is for psychotics.

Holding shame to save others from madness causes you to go further down in disgust/sadness.

It's an over-responsibility to hold onto shame. Dont over-give but stand up/walk in your lane.

When you see who you are you won't take on the weight of the world--the projections of others girl.

Using your imagination is vital to healing. Envision giving back shame to the original being.

Imagine or mentally rehearse the shame leaving your body and going back into the giver Jane.

This imagining reminds you: "Oh, that's not who I am--it's an improper mirror/a trip laid on too."

You are now free to love, since shame blocks love of self and others. It's a life/relationship destroyer.

It also blocks love of God. You can't love fully if blocked by toxic shame and besides we're all flawed.

You can't love yourself if filled with toxic shame and any other love is not forthcoming or little gain.

TAMING OF THE INSTINCTS

You're sensitive, you have gifts, you're an empath--and look what happens to people like this.

Sibling rivalry is natural but must be curbed lest it become malicious, often even devilish.

Preface: GIFTS BRING RIFTS

Before one makes gold on desire--before he has it under control--he's not a king but a peon/loser.

Self-mastery of the instincts: that's what defines the knight. Being a slave to tastes is a blight.

I had to learn this cuz I was wild. I couldn't get enough but lacked style, weak not tough/easily riled.

From wanting to eat everything in the universe to fasting and going inward to spiritual experiences.

I now live totally in the right brain. I do this, I do that and putter all day long, nothing planned.

PROPLE PROJECT THEIR CRAP

People project crap onto you. Without good boundaries or maturity we take on that view.

If immature/undeveloped we feel shame for what they project we are and it starts from there.

Imagine: They've done something but WE feel shame for it--that's the matrix and don't forget it.

Example: A woman is violently raped and she's to blame for it--it's ridiculous and primitive.

They project their evil thoughts on us and we take it on as our identity--a lifelong shame matrix.

It became an entire personality trait having nothing to do with me--demons entered in too see.

Not only do they project their crap they gossip to others about it as if it's all true the dirt's in YOU.

They act like you're insane/crazy when you're just being normal: you switch to be comfortable.

43

Preface: GIFTS BRING RIFTS

FRANTIC SEARCH FOR PEACE

I frantically searched for the way to act which would avoid their wrath and that was that.

How does an undeveloped psych know he's in a crazy world? He doesn't/just becomes ill.

So that's how the altered, abnormal personality develops: it FITS the awaiting insane matrix.

The basis of mental illness is other people's projections--other people are the problem.

Acting in a certain way to avoid punishment, that silly ineffectual style became obdurate.

It scares me just to think about it: the incorporation of others, in like an internal melting pot.

Pray to God to take everything outa your spirit not of Him and you. Evil ghosts, not just a few.

We took on behaviors to avoid punishment and they hardened as our style but are no good.

SHE'S GUILTY FOR WHAT HE'S THINKING

A woman is called "dirty" for what the man is thinking. This is the matrix I'm describing.

He took one look at her and wanted her. Then she was called a harlot, homewrecker, adulterer.

In adolescence she blossomed, sister was threatened and projected her crap so she caved in.

Born whole and clear, we mal-adapt to the system which awaits us and it's mean/ridiculous.

Preface: GIFTS BRING RIFTS

Nothing crueler than a woman's wrath and what they do to each other is tragic/not just sass.

The minute I moved to town the women sized me up and hated me, an army bringing me down.

I was already traumatized by the two feminists sisters era, I wasn't ready for another drama.

When two evil sisters collude with bad mother against female empath younger it's a Cinderella.

I developed crutches to deal with the mixed up signals and that incited more of these devils.

You gotta make gold on your mal-adaptations to others. These are crutches, little "helpers".

CRUTCHES BRING MORE ATTACKS

If not ready to let crutches go then your life comes to blows from those in your circle.

You gotta become a knight: let crutches go, stand up to and boundary demons coming at you.

Crutches incite more attacks. We are weakened by em and the shrewd move in for supply/sex.

When demons creeped into my house I was too weak and the invasion put me up a creek.

Unless a young woman is fully prepared and coached she'll be sucked up into an evil vortex.

I dare to say most girls are molested by age ten. It's a weird, indecent, devilish era we live in.

Swept up into an evil vortex while being in denial and even encouraged by those we know.

Preface: GIFTS BRING RIFTS

I'll be dead when most read this but I assert it's the basis: being imposed on = neuroses.

Jezebel left him off in my house to wait but it was just like putting a rattlesnake in my cage.

It's important to watch your thoughts and cut the dross: they're often implants from others.

Constant and intense shame: was this not an implant from the sister who hated you--Jane?

This was Jane, this was me. This was mom and that was gossip from her bridge club see.

So they call you rude/a hater/antisocial for not letting em in--simply close the door girlfriend.

I've been there, I understand all this and it was horrible--the impositions of other people.

EMPATH HYPERSENSITIVE/BOUNDARIES

For an empath hypersensitive it's a drain and strain to go out as you're picking up on thoughts.

They get to see you, just cuz they WANT to? No more of that, a hostess to sick environments.

You're no more a slave to the social: the biggest way Satan gets in and makes you act coocoo.

You wanna be a cocoon protected against the coocoo. Draw your domain/set boundaries for YOU.

For jealousy is the MAJOR human emotion. It is cruel, compulsive, primitive and murderous too.

That's why they hate you. If rich I'd act humble, not flaunt it, the communist spirit will kill you.

Preface: GIFTS BRING RIFTS

Born whole & clear we meet a buzz-saw. Chopped up in pieces, distorted, made into something odd.

MONEY SOLVES ALL THINGS

Money just flows thru your hands. And don't have those people around, those bloodsuckers/men.

When I had lotsa money I just spent it. That alone showed immaturity when it came to finances.

For the queen makes herself financially independent. She doesn't take wild chances or spend it.

Otherwise you must depend on man/move in with him. Disaster follows when not staying alone.

Move in with a man, lose your independence and power base. This is hellish, I'll never forget it ok.

It was the stupidest thing I ever did and til my dying breath I'm amazed I ever took that step.

When I arrived his friends entered the room: in sudden terror I saw I'd lost my protective cocoon.

That's an extreme example of what's happening to all to a different degree: influences on thee.

ONLY INDEPENDENCE IS FREEDOM

My Lord woman, stay alone if you can--til God brings your husband and his anointed protection.

And don't let a man in your house! He could attack you when inside so where do you get off?

Wicked men creep into a house and take a woman captive due to weakness and diverse lusts.

Preface: GIFTS BRING RIFTS

When meeting professionally, stay task-oriented and don't get involved beyond that definitely.

Don't allow early traumas to enter or his thoughts about her just focus on the task before us.

Then get back to the pad and be happy you have a trusting spouse and a life: true reality.

Be a cocoon amongst the coocoo: be that now forever to co-create with God, the most clever.

HATED FOR BEING DIFFERENT

They were so rude and insulting without knowing me--who wouldn't want to be alone/FREE?

This is how it works: they already hated you for being different so then capitalized on your quirks.

That was my Waterloo, the hill I had to die on: having to live with misjudgments, no explanation.

"I don't wanna get involved" is the healthy reaction but I had not yet learned the greatest lesson.

And now with the invasion of diverse elements a woman can't be talked into things/must grow up.

How does a unique genius explain to dummies who he is? He stays cheerful til his ship comes in.

If you're arguing you're devolving. That's no longer my thing: I'll wait for God's husband for me.

The invaders call your insistence on privacy "rudeness" or anti-social hatred-- a ploy to see.

I'm a sensitive artist: creative self-expressor. In the past this sensitivity was a self-destructor.

Preface: GIFTS BRING RIFTS

I'm lucky to be alive. I took chances with bad characters because they prey on the naive.

Filthy projections: Instead of catching them in the moment we say "I've gotta calm down".

Gaslighting is a process: it's when you start apologizing for crap projected onto your highness.

Without knowledge of humans in their social world you may sink in your swill cuz you didn't know.

I had no idea what people were like. I surmised nice boys then was destroyed by evil teens, aye.

Held hostage by presumed friendship. "We're acquaintances, there's a difference" I shoulda said.

STOP ANCHORING BACKWARD

After working it all thru stop looking back cuz it's an anchor to low levels in the painful past.

When taking a stand against evil is called rudeness or anti-social it proof what I'm talking about.

Get a hobby or some other past time to wash the inherited, unwarranted, implanted shame out.

Tho' emotions are pained from projections spewed upon you like sewage you smile/get thru it.

When they project their low emotional intelligence on you turn it back onto those with low IQ.

A true queen doesn't brag, she just struts her stuff: here's my project, take it or leave it.

He got her back in the worst way: he withdrew his protection then a right to his station.

Preface: GIFTS BRING RIFTS

The most productive time is looking out the window and pondering not stuffing information in.

His attention never went beyond himself. As for being interested in me as a person, no skill set.

You feel you don't exist with a narcissist. He's no interest in what you think/feel, no skill set.

In your season of treason you learn very quickly you can't trust anyone even your own kin.

You were protected in a castle/household and now have been cast out. Divorce can feel like that.

Normalcy: We harmonize despite our differences but that's not possible with narcissists.

RIGID HIERARCHIES ARE HELL SEE

Narcs grew to a rigid hierarchy so feel insecure very easily: Am I enough? Do people respect me?

The best way to soothe their inner tensions is to dominate--that's the groove to ego-inflate.

The games keep coming in their domination system so we must be ready to stand up to them.

They're not interested in your input or "nuance". It's an authoritarian system they come with sis.

He's not interested in complexity: the name of the game is his opinion only, no time to dilly-dally.

They pontificate: by declaring here's the way it has to be and either do it or sink in your swill see.

His game is "shut up". You keep disparate opinions to yourself, they're not welcome here at all.

Preface: GIFTS BRING RIFTS

If you disagree it's shut up--you're invalid. There are many invalidation messages in this set up.

His words of condescension clearly indicate he won't hear from you lest you're in lock step.

No figuring things out, no teasing out subtle differences--it's all listen to me you stooges.

His third game is: You'll Be Sorry. Punishment for individuation is how they engage see.

His 4th tactic is humiliation: bringing others into the game in embarrassing public declaration.

He's not satisfied to shut you down, he incites others with the same contempt all over town.

They author misinformation and smear campaigns full of distortion, they wreck your reputation.

You go against me and there's gonna be a big price to pay: the whole world is gonna know ok.

IMMEDIATE PUNISHMENTS FOR DISSIDENCE

His immediate punishment is passive aggression, evasion, withdrawal. I've got nothing for you gal.

"Let's work on this as a team": silence, nonparticipation, won't return calls/do as promised.

The stubborn nonparticipation style comes after saying he's glad to work with such a great gal.

His next style is "I've got people". He attracts authoritarians living vicariously thru his evil.

The more people he combines into his groupthink the more pressure is on you to conform see.

Preface: GIFTS BRING RIFTS

If you don't think like "us" you become the outsider, the outlier--then things get worse from there.

They will not quit. Give em trouble and they'll double down on these tactics. Reject/avoid it.

Identifying his games is ultra essential. You must have boundaries to recall who you are at all.

Having your own ideas means you won't have a coordinated life with him, so why try ma'am?

If you go with him realize you won't have closeness and it'll require many personal adjustments.

Narcissists are game players. Life to them is competition--win or lose--and you're the loser.

After this mess you'll want to move on to relationships where the game isn't rigged in advance.

RECAP: SHAMERS ARE DOUBLESPEAK

The perpetrators of shame are full of doublespeak. They are insincere, untrustworthy leaks.

They're like leftists who say you're too dumb so they must speak for you. It's being owned too.

Liberals: if you don't think like them in lockstep they'll come to your house like Kavanaugh.

Been gone six years now, what a relief outa that poverty-stricken police state of liberal hate.

I've stopped watching the news because it's the same old blues: by gov we're being screwed.

Stop stuffing information from the outside in and start evoking your OWN thing from within.

Preface: GIFTS BRING RIFTS

Look out the window and muse, that's a better use of your time. It's an inside job I'm saying.

The seed has been predestined in you, just clarify by repenting of habits recycling energy in lieu.

Self-control is a fruit of the spirit but sad to say these days few men have it: sensual lunatics.

Is it variety or austerity which increases longevity? Man is oligophagous, existing on fewest varieties.

A humble lifestyle has few varieties. Total monotony defines the saints and their great longevity.

A wild profligate lifestyle has endless variety for stuffing. The saints go inward, not gorging.

Safely encased in the bosom of monotony the saints could go inward to many mansions see.

GIFTS BRING RIFTS

IT HURTS TO LET EM GO, BUT...

If you think independently prepare to be alone for this
generation is the most conformist ever known.

If you adapt to losers you lose your vibrancy--then you
hang on more as if you need their guidance, see?

They'll attack for not doing what they want, so of
course they'll hate if you think higher than a grunt.

The mentally effete fall into the popular groove but
some see it as crude (always in a feud)--is that you?

They're so empty they cling to you but then try to
control to maintain their comfort zone too.

There is no bigger influence/addiction than people in
your life. They eclipse your destiny and cause strife.

It hurts to let em go but if you do a whole new vista
opens up to you--a fantastic cornucopia so true.

GHOSTING IS RUDE

UTTER LONELINESS CONQUERED
I JUST WANTED TO BE ALONE!
ONE SIDED FRIENDSHIPS
FRIENDSHIPS TAKE WORK LAZY
YOUR EXCITEMENT IS FLATTENED
GHOSTING CAUSES UNCERTAINTY
ENDING IT MEANS ENDING IT
GHOSTING IS RUDE BUT DON'T USE FOOD
ESSENTIAL SELF-FORGIVENESS
A WEAK VESSEL FOR DEVIL: ADDICTION
FOOD MEANS MOTHER
GET INVOLVED AND GO DOWN
SELF-FORGIVENESS CUES DESTINY!

GIFTS BRING RIFTS

THE SMART ARE ALONE
IT HURTS TO LET EM GO, BUT...
SHAME FEELS INGRAINED
SHAME: IT WASN'T YOU
YOU WEREN'T GOOD ENOUGH!
MARRIAGE IS PROTECTION
FEMALE GENIUS TARGTED BY THUGS
MUST CLOSE THE DOOR!
GHOSTING IS RUDE!
DON'T TELL ME TO CONFORM TO ROT
AVOID THE ENERGY-SUCKERS
PEOPLE WERE SANE IN THE FIFTIES
ARTE YOU ATTRACTING THESE FOOLS?
TWO BLOCKS TO SUCCESS: SIN AND FRIENDS
ADAPTING TO LEFTISTS OR THE LEFT-BRAIN
STAY AWAY FROM FEMINISTS
OF COURSE THEY TELL YOU TO SHARE
ONLY ONE GOD-CHOSEN LINK
AS A LIBERAL I KNEW IT ALL TOO
SORRY, I HAVE TO LET YOU GO

GIFTS BRING RIFTS

JEZEBEL SPIRITS LOVE TO TAKE OVER
WE ALWAYS HAVE THE ADVERSARY
ALCOHOL-DRUGS AND LOWER CHARACTERS
COMING OUTA YOUR SHELL
GOD OVERTURNS FALSE IMAGES OF YOU
SEX IS ALL THEY THINK ABOUT
DECOMPENSATION AND COLLAPSED IDENTITY
ALL ANIMALS ADAPT TO ENVIRONMENT
THE SPIRIT OF ESTHER
THINKING IT'S ALL GOOD
LIKE A TSUNAMI
IT'S THE STYLE TO HATE TRUMP
PASSWORD TO GOD'S BLESSINGS: THANKS!
LET GOD FILL IN THE STEPS
I'M GONNA ENJOY WAITING FOR GOD
REAL SUCCESS IS A TIDAL WAVE
FOOD AND CHEMICAL OBSTRUCTIONS
BREAD, BUTTER AND FRUIT ONCE ONLY
RAW MILK MACHINE

GHOSTING IS RUDE

UTTER LONELINESS CONQUERED

I solved the terrible homesick problem by living alone in the desert wilderness in a tiny cabin.

I fruitlessly remained on the fruit diet but only regained mental health by adding cheese to it.

Suddenly, like a light switch, all orthorexic fears were gone and that ugly green demon never returned.

Cheese, fruit, pomegranate juice. Utter simplicity in a cabin experiencing exploding inner universe.

I was joyous, like newness. Now the problem was intruders [frenemies] making me crazy and pissed.

It took me years to get over the PTSD from intrusive memories of the intruders, my frenemies.

I JUST WANTED TO BE ALONE!

After living in my tiny universe it was like a cantankerous tidal wave imposing on me, my frenemies.

I can't get over how you invaded my solitude with your friend then left him like I was a bus station.

I won't forget how you invade my privacy to charge phone & use bathroom like I'm a gas station.

GIFTS BRING RIFTS

I can't forget how you talk thru music or other annoying left-brain, grey, boring characteristics.

Imagine living in a small trailer then suddenly a crowd comes in. That's how it felt having friends.

They can't forgive you so you can't forgive yourself? Come on, a necessity isn't socially-based.

The ongoing shame was socially based: they wanted me down, have me not go forward head-on.

There's something called Inherited Shame too: the system's need to scapegoat one not two.

The sickening thing is the effect of shame on soul ties where you're being used as meat by a guy.

Plumbing: that's all you are girl. Get that through your pretty head and prepare to be dead.

ONE SIDED FRIENDSHIPS

Sick relationships take many forms. Some don't gossip, lie or outright hurt-- just flake out.

A good friend listens with empathy but in a one-sided friendship it's all about them/their crises.

Once you begin they tune out quickly or turn the conversation back on them instantly.

They don't open up or share much. There's always secrecy and things feel so unbalanced.

They don't share nor open up you see, so your interactions fall flat or feel incomplete.

Suddenly they're gone and you ask yourself: what have I done wrong? It's them not you hon'

GIFTS BRING RIFTS

Support from friends makes a big difference in times of distress but it's absence makes you worse.

Their consistent failure to reciprocate [when you need it most] frustrates and hurts. Caution: escape.

FRIENDSHIPS TAKE WORK LAZY

Friendship takes work and healthy communication is how but if there's no reciprocation, wow.

It's normal to be upset by unbalanced relationships and you aren't needy for wanting more kid.

Emotional turmoil results after they say they care but their consistent disinterest triggers terror.

A balanced friendship strengthens feelings of belonging and self-worth not this kind of hurt.

Feeling the cold triggers worry you've offended, lack social talent or are just flatly rejected.

Anxieties make you avoid other friends for fear of driving them away too, you're just inferior Sue.

This negative self-talk can damage your self-esteem but it comes with the territory it seems.

Recurrently they reinforce your faith in their commitment ["thinking of you"] but that's only temporary too.

YOUR EXCITEMENT IS FLATTENED

They ask for help and this shift flattens your excitement for these users of the moment.

They quickly fall back into their habit of failing to respond and now you're back to doubt.

GIFTS BRING RIFTS

Their cold behavior triggers memories of other failed relationships causing more disappointment.

It's natural to want strong friendships for isolation can cause serious mental consequences.

But a friend with little consideration of your emotional needs will not ease the loneliness see.

Your emotional support requires energy and if nothing in return it depletes and you're not free.

GHOSTING CAUSES UNCERTAINTY

Their ghosting caused uncertainty, loss of self-confidence and now you can't trust.

If the pattern re-emerges of sudden disappearances after two weeks I'd question the bond sis.

Always recall you ended it cuz it caused you pain. Getting back in touch says it's ok, do it again.

You may now recognize the "friendship" for what it is and hey, you don't really care! But beware.

Instead of promoting happy connection, one-sided friendships create distress and resentment.

Friendships don't always thrive no matter how much time, energy and love you inject, aye.

Ending things releases you to victory. Up to now it's been a sorry story so get good at this honey.

ENDING IT MEANS ENDING IT

Once you end it, stop reaching out. Stick with your decision even when missing them: ouch.

GIFTS BRING RIFTS

Like other interpersonal skills being a friend takes trial and error or the commitment is insincere.

True friends accept help when they need it but make sure to offer you the same: remember this.

GHOSTING IS RUDE BUT DON'T USE FOOD

They hated Princess Di/Jackie Kennedy for Queen's Disease so if you had it you're in good company.

Bulimia is characterized--defined by--SHAME. So use the Princess Di archetype of Grande Dame.

She was edacious from early trauma but couldn't afford to weigh 600 pounds so got caught up sir.

Princess Dia was edacious from marital/jealousy and betrayal trauma while escaping the drama.

I was edacious because I had a homesick feeling in my gut until it was filled again but then what?

So homesick for self and God they use addictions to get along but now they gotta forgive themselves.

ESSENTIAL SELF-FORGIVENESS

I eat for sustenance and to quiet hunger pains. Not for emotional needs, that'll never happen again.

Just say: yes they treated me unkindly but I'll put it all behind me cuz I was really bad too you see.

Just two weeks of SRIs in my 20s affected me for decades esp if I ever got drunk--they're bunk.

SRIs made me a crazy mama, I went to teach my class in pajamas, my lowest phase and trauma.

GIFTS BRING RIFTS

SRIs are anti-depressants or anti-psychotics and they'll both bloat you up and make you lunatic.

I was so insane there is no behavior I can account for but big pharma's pills threw me to the floor.

It's hard self-forgiving behavior I can't account for but it's all the past bag to resolve/discard.

I was nuts, in a rut, immature, didn't know what's what, in a dump half the time, started getting drunk.

A WEAK VESSEL FOR DEVIL: ADDICTION

God forgave me for addictive devices I used to deal with early trauma [whatever it was with mama].

The bad results of alcohol on a hypersensitive took up the next few decades as a relapser.

I was so homesick for I knew not what, all I knew was misery in a crowd and I began seeking God.

I matured in the desert after my early life of constant mishaps. I loved solitude in deep thought.

I became enraptured in my solitude and miserable when invaded by frenemies--then I began to see.

Alcoholism progresses even while sober. You're clean for five years then pick it up = utter disaster.

Been sober 25 years and scared of the stuff. The last time I drank I went baseline, it's rough.

FOOD MEANS MOTHER

Food means mother and other devices mean mistress: addiction takes first place and its serious.

GIFTS BRING RIFTS

I don't mind telling you this cuz it can relieve your stress. You're not alone, we're all feeling lost.

I had so much stress built up in my body it cracked like a vase one day and I cried like a crazy baby.

My whole body was clenched up in abreaction, frozen just as I was silenced by the sick system.

Don't commit to friends where you're roped into things or if they pressure you to--need solitude.

Everyone she involved me with hurt me deeply. That's a clear sign of friendship inferiority see.

GET INVOLVED AND GO DOWN

Get involved and go down an evil rabbit hole. Stay home instead, have a great day that's all.

Never go anywhere with someone unless husband. You lose control and they may start abusin'.

You can't explain to the dumb so stop trying hon'. You're a genius so how to explain to them?

Being married to Ray was like having the sheriff as my right hand and my life took on from then.

Women love to get you in the car and take control, taking you everywhere you don't wanna go.

My prescription for you is to never leave home. Stop wasting time while being fully in control.

Look at the Ukranians--the horrors of losing home. Love it while you still can never to roam.

Feminism degraded the home cuz they wanted to go out but there's nothing there, it's all inner gal.

GIFTS BRING RIFTS

Also seek forgiveness for all the stuff you did with the devil in you, when he was in control Sue.

Even though it wasn't you but the devil coming through you, it's was weakness that got you.

You gotta stay strong to keep this crap away. Bad associations, entities and false ideologies.

SELF-FORGIVENESS CUES DESTINY!

I'll go more into self-forgiveness in the next book. It's ultra important or your destiny is blocked.

It was hard to forgive myself cuz I was such an extremist in whatever I did, good or bad it was intense.

Just as I purposed to write 100 plus books, extreme energy can go the other way: mad kooks.

Creativity must go somewhere. It's either creative self-expression or [creative] self-destruction sir.

Kindly teach this to the youth so they don't waste decades needlessly like I did or perhaps you.

GIFTS BRING RIFTS

THE SMART ARE ALONE

If you think independently prepare to be alone for this generation is the most conformist ever known.

If you adapt to losers you lose your vibrancy--then you hang on more as if you need their guidance, see?

They'll attack for not doing what they want, so of course they'll hate if you think higher than a grunt.

The mentally effete fall into the popular groove but some see it as crude (always in a feud)--is that you?

They're so empty they cling to you but then try to control to maintain their comfort zone too.

There is no bigger influence/addiction than people in your life. They eclipse your destiny and cause strife.

IT HURTS TO LET EM GO, BUT...

It hurts to let em go but if you do a whole new vista opens up to you--a fantastic cornucopia so true.

Stop looking at your numbers, it's all about the right LINK. Let these losers (evil helpers) go--they stink!

ANYTHING genius does is criticized. Genius is always different and novel while they've been cut to size.

To be happy you must face what genius is. It's the OPPOSITE to mundaneity so it makes them pissed.

If they're not 100% for your destiny/what you do, let em go. They're not what God wants for you ya know.

You're the top 10%, born to be winners. What are you doing with these losers holding you down/sinners?

It's all about you: Every time you don't go back it's another notch in your belt as you learn to eschew.

GIFTS BRING RIFTS

Go back and it gives a bottomfeeder a chance to take you way UP or way DOWN making you the clown.

SHAME FEELS INGRAINED

Shame is an intensely painful feeling that we are flawed and therefore unworthy of love and belonging.

Guilt: "I did wrong". Shame: "I AM wrong". The shamed one suffers lack of connection which worsens.

Shame feels powerful and ingrained. You've done plenty wrong but you feel wrong as a person, stained.

Shame both precedes and results from bulimia. Even after recovery shame completely runs ya.

Shamed as a child then an event occurs as the symptoms roll out then more shame from connections lost.

Shame drives sensitives to discount the bad image. To not be driven under they become famous.

It was either succeed and inevitably be famous OR be seen as crazy, nutty, weird, inferior, an ass.

It was either Do Your Thing or be driven under with the severe undertow of the dumbed down public.

Only genius sees genius, the rest think he's ridiculous--they aren't educated to see him for what he is.

I just always marched to a different drummer--in my room with hobbies, projects and new learning tools.

Since the boomers it's been about the SOCIAL and partying. I have always found it totally boring.

There are no tools to deal with shame other than Christ whose atonement covered it--it was erased.

GIFTS BRING RIFTS

SHAME: IT WASN'T YOU

It helps the shame bearer to know they were a radically different person and the devil was the author.

Being a recluse makes it harder and easier to overcome shame. If alone, it helps to self-congratulate.

I have never met such bores as socially-minded people who are terrified of stepping on toes.

When you step on toes from telling the truth don't let disconnections increase shame, just do it.

Shame led to bulimia but veganism ignited the crap--when adding cheese she recovered just like that.

Recovered bulimics are usually very nice ladies who feel shame for past disgusting behavior for life.

That's why shame is something only Christ can cure. And also knowing it's demons possessing the girl.

For the shamed bulimic may also be a kleptomaniac or a whore since it's demonic possession by a fort.

Only Jesus can erase it then it's at the deepest part of the sea and He puts a sign up "don't go fishing here".

YOU WEREN'T GOOD ENOUGH!

When they decided you weren't good enough and ghosted you, you took the blame, didn't you?

No need gossip, the final arbiter is God and He saw/heard everything you did/said, you're dead.

I don't have to get em on my side, GOD is the arbiter and He sees your chicaneries you vicious gossiper.

GIFTS BRING RIFTS

Wicked always hang together like peas in a pod. Don't feel vulnerable cuz alone you're fortified by God.

Go ahead, do your social/fans/popular routine, I'm not keen. I think beyond this corny world, I SEE.

Mentor Jenna says not texting back is rude and disrespectful and man, that was a true earful.

MARRIAGE IS PROTECTION

The. crazy feminists say "marriage is captivity" but no ma'am, marriage is FREEDOM/protection.

The minute I got married all my problems stopped. No one invading me, pressuring me: I WAS FREE.

Before marriage I was invaded by men/women alike and it was hell. Young or old, I was targeted still.

This wasn't a big city it was a small desert town of liberals and ne'er-do-wells who could steal and no jail.

The cops wouldn't protect me due to the ACLU protecting these little thugs, idle/slothful people: "slugs".

FEMALE GENIUS TARGTED BY THUGS

One of em was town slut with her army of flying monkeys warring on anyone she saw as an enemy.

City thugs are going into small towns and taking over. You don't ever hear about this but how I suffered!

My one fear is being single again. Unless I went into a convent but I'd be hounded/pressured even then.

Women need men to protect them and if they deny that they're just plain dense/hypnotized/blind as bats.

GIFTS BRING RIFTS

University tried to push me into therapy due to "feeling the need for protection" cuz it's all good man.

MUST CLOSE THE DOOR!

You are NOT going to hurt me anymore like this. I'm closing the door and will not be a recidivist.

For love hurts SO much, yet it shouldn't. It doesn't have to but with us it's been the pits, hasn't it?

I'm closing the door cuz life is too short/I'm too smart/fabulous to suffer, and suffer some more.

So take your insufferable ideas and besides-the-point rants and I'll return to what makes sense.

I was ALL-OK before I met you, so forget you. God is more important than people and He said NO.

What you've done to my self-esteem is shocking. Just by me having you in my focus I was degrading.

When over I'll feel much better. It MAY hurt for awhile but I'll bite this bullet and overcome the messer.

NO CONTACT: Every time you don't go back you grow in fact and for every time you give in: sad sack.

GHOSTING IS RUDE!

Ghosting is rude. I know it hurts but don't allow petty bottom feeders in your life and you're cured.

High level worth: a creative act. Low level worth: My identity depends on whether I'm texed by an idiot.

Face it: Ghosting is rude and a sign of poor character. You want a loving soul not one who disappears.

GIFTS BRING RIFTS

She's nice but not there 100%. She flakes out recurrently and it's always hard to take, curious, discrepant.

As long as she's my friend I'm up and down depending on her reactions which are narrow and dumb.

I had to let her go lest my world shrink without a halo. I'd rather be alone than wonder what she's up to now.

Stick to what you believe no matter how silly, unprofessional or useless they call your work God conceived.

They've been trained to conform to the norm and didn't have the audacity to object like you: the storm!

God says get outa My way with petty plans and stay away from losers calling themselves professionals!

DON'T TELL ME TO CONFORM TO ROT

Don't tell me you can help me cuz you CANNOT. You want me to conform to the norm which is ROT.

I will never seek earthly help again. It's so insulting to face their abuse called "advice" backed by nothing.

They wanna put me and God's work through the ringer and it's one big insult to this great discoverer.

You reach a point of being so hurt you just give up. That's when destiny breaks open--so look up!

Once they're gone your whole world opens up UNLESS you keep resentments churning non-stop.

I was so weak from sin I was defenseless when the losers flowed in--I let em in then they did me in.

Recall no good deed ever goes unpunished. Be good to them but don't expect love like dogs or cats.

GIFTS BRING RIFTS

Ask: Are they for me or against me? Are they friends who manipulate you to be who they want you to be?

I don't need your poison going into my spirit. I'll love ya from afar but getting closer to you? I fear it.

I had to shut em all out just to think. They are ceaseless in their jabbering and socializing, so rinky-dink!

Let em all go from your mind. Be thorough: as if you never met em--those conformists so unkind.

AVOID THE ENERGY-SUCKERS

They are energy-suckers. You spend one hour with them and you've run a marathon. Goodbye, son!

You've done something magnificent and original. "They" call it corny and stupid cuz it's unconventional.

Not only do they drain the energy outa you they criticize the novel and unique and you're left blue.

You can't spend your life pulling them UP without spoiling your God-given destiny: reject then pushup.

It's rare that a genius can create and be a social creature too. There's bound to be problems to chew.

Stop explaining to them cuz they'll never understand and it weakens your position/makes you look bad.

Let em go: pay them off. Be nice as you walk away cuz people are cruel: you need rest after a ripoff.

Rest after ripoff: They all took advantage but now you know--those who are dumbed will also scoff.

Get use to solitude cuz NO ONE can really approve or disapprove. You are the creator not those fools.

GIFTS BRING RIFTS

I worked in the back of a ghost town for 27 years. I woulda done anything to get some peace after tears.

Whoever has a destiny will be bothered constantly. Expect Satan's obstruction by calling you "unfriendly".

You're not one of them, you won't adapt. You stand out--novel and unique--and that they can't accept.

The worst is going "out" with them. Now you're a slave to idiocy and good luck getting back to your den.

After being carted around like cargo to their many stops, I never went again and that's my good luck.

PEOPLE WERE SANE IN THE FIFTIES

People were sane in the fifties but now they're debauched and crazy so I say just stay home Missy.

I felt so free, happy and relieved getting rid of all my "professional" helpers who destroyed my dreams!

What do you they know, just cuz they're "professionals"? Creative genius is not the same as "tech skills".

The greatest artists are scientists and the greatest scientists are artists--a realm way above their petty skills.

This generation is so lost in sensual past times/thoughts they could never really create, the hedonists.

How could debauched losers with technical skills advise genius--it gives me chills and is ridiculous.

God gave you such a major destiny it's surprising anyone can relate. Escape bad fate, alone you're great.

You wanna help people but can't be around em. That's what it's all come to after being confounded.

73

GIFTS BRING RIFTS

Nothing they do makes sense cuz it's situational ethics. It's point-by-point not God's plan and magic.

If they're gonna do anything and have no lines. how can these "professionals" help you, the refined?

As iron sharpens iron one friend sharpens another. Are your friends irritating you or making you stronger?

They make you compromise--that's the very worst part of the "grievance and entitlement" politics.

Letting em in was your first mistake. After that it was an imposition and terrible situation by those fakes.

ARE YOU ATTRACTING THESE FOOLS?

Why do they come over to bother you? Cuz losers have nothing better to do and are needy and blue.

It's all SOCIAL to the hangout generation and thus your happy independence is the worst of all to em.

The fact you're so happy without them makes them madder than hell: You're a hater living in a shell.

With them around I stuttered trying not to offend. It was exhausting and I'm so glad to be rid of em.

Every time I was with him/her I became worse than before--that's a toxic relationship to the core.

Look at it as a poisoning. Where you do business, play ball or be with earthlings makes you LESS, see?

Liberal feminist women have the narrowest threshold limits. You go over em and you'll wish you hadn't.

You may be too high and exalted for your generation. Be more polite to do good with the errant.

GIFTS BRING RIFTS

Life is too short, your time too valuable and your destiny too great to waste any more time or it's bad fate!

In the land of the blind the one-eyed man is king. So we learn to respect this one guy to whom we cling.

Get the true barometer--study kings, genius and saints of old--and leave this era behind to find the gold.

In the old days kids were mature by 12. Now they're still living with parents who are quickly getting old.

TWO BLOCKS TO SUCCESS: SIN AND FRIENDS

The two blocks to success are habits (sin) and friends (bad associations)--think hard on that my friends.

I'm not gonna spend it with people who are constantly pulling me down draining my life energy: no more!

They ask rude, impertinent questions thinking they have a right to--like your age, weight or income too.

In an ageist culture they use your age to put you down. Asking how old you are is rude, so don't tell em.

They're jealous of your status but could never do all that you did to get it so forget the herd: so be it.

The emergent politics is Grievance and Entitlement--so very destructive, why would you want this?

If you don't speak the new politics they're gonna attack you, the best. Refuse the new pronouns of twits.

Don't ever seek their approval or appreciation or be disappointed. Seek God's and you'll be anointed.

Stop letting people use you as a pit stop. You've been on their daily run for far too long: resist then look UP.

GIFTS BRING RIFTS

If you're afraid of his reaction ask: is he the right attraction? Is he helping your dreams or against em?

I'm afraid of his reaction cuz I know he doesn't understand genius--the Creative may seem ridiculous.

She wants the furniture moved here, then there, then back again--that's the creative process my friend.

When she's working with a tech guy the creative process is likely to be seen as crazy female vacillating.

ADAPTING TO LEFTISTS OR THE LEFT-BRAIN

I understand that so don't ask too much--even tho' I'm paying him to experiment with a hunch.

That's why I should learn code--to compromise with confusion in another the design always suffers.

I can't give up my designs just cuz helpers are lost or unrefined--this is my destiny so I keep tryin'.

I'm done with amateur creativity-stunters callilng themselves professionals, so full of themselves.

Don't ever hand over your work to them! Only the tried-and-true can work with you the rest create bedlam.

Common sense is catching in America--it isn't cuz you're a lesbian I don't like you it's your tyranny over us.

I don't dislike you cuz you're a lessie but because you're a thin-skinned witch seeking only tyranny.

I think you're a jezebel witch not cuz you're a lesbian but due to your false viewpoints and dominance!

You're trying to take our free speech away while implanting your disgusting and dirty theories of the day.

GIFTS BRING RIFTS

STAY AWAY FROM FEMINISTS

In some weird twisted man-hating crap feminists cozied up to Islam's alpha males, can you believe that?

Common sense is popular and these women are a bunch of cackling witches restricting our freedom.

Your son rebels against you witch cuz he wants freedom like all good people who turn against evil.

Teenage boys are waking up to freedom and their feminist mothers are rebelling by blocking/bashing em.

They're actually corporate fascists masquerading as liberals working with establishment for the censorship.

Stupid crazy witch women trying to take our freedoms: Stop ruining your young sons waking up to you, madams!

OF COURSE THEY TELL YOU TO SHARE

They tell you to "share" cuz they want what you have. Dare to disappoint demanders/the arrogant.

You are just gonna have to let em go for they are pulling you down and that's all you need to know.

Above all avoid the youth--except rare exceptions standing for decency, goodness, freedom, truth.

For youth have been deliberately dumbed down, blinded and sexualized--that's all they think about.

They know nothing & refuse to learn anything especially not facing the irrational basis of their theories.

Thank God a writer doesn't have to see anyone--he's defined by his copy living eternally after his death.

GIFTS BRING RIFTS

I got so tired of his coming over! I'm not social--just wanna work or putter--
and he was such a bore.

It hurt so much when I had to adapt to others--not in control--and now to not
have to--WOW, WOW, WOW!

Spouse and I live in two separate buildings on the same site. Now that is total
luxury and how we love it!

For an artist or writer or thinker, NOTHING beats being alone. If you can do it
together, life is full blown.

ONLY ONE GOD-CHOSEN LINK

There's ONE God-chosen link and an infinite number of non-links so now just
relax and don't even pick.

I reward my team cuz there's so few on it. The world has been dumbed down
but I love what's around.

I would never put all those chemicals and fillers (called "Bakery") into my body
again. It was HELL/a sin.

Stop searching for mind entertainment on the net. You want TRIGGERS for
your own thoughts, the best.

After holding it in for years--being speech-suppressed--I long to express myself
to the messed up.

I was bashed for my expressions for decades when they ruled: liberals
dumbing us down to be fools.

Give up on them: they've done nothing but take your money and confuse you.
God's got it--He's so cool!

I long to bash em back: articulately/intellectually of course cuz I'm prepared
to confront the curse.

My work stands on its own, I don't have to see anyone. I've had it, I just wanna
retire into riches/MON.

GIFTS BRING RIFTS

To think after 40 years unremunerated hard work I'd go on The View to defend it to those shrews? Uh, NO.

I've given you the formula and shown them to be empty, filthy and stupid just for votes/TYRANNY over people.

They are cruel because they are negligent. They are horrible because they are empty-headed: cold, spent.

Do you think I would face that cruel witch Behar or Whoopi? Liberals act like they know everything.

AS I LIBERAL I KNEW IT ALL TOO

I felt I KNEW IT ALL too as a liberal. We all were by default, in those years when it was taken for granted.

It took three days in bed/excruciating pain to survive the Wallmart Bakery experiment and I gained.

The old cat is noisy and hisses constantly cuz she's had it--and thus takes dominance over dogs.

After outdoors in cold with other animals and being owned by an angry female now Old Cats Rule.

I'm sorry I'm just too bored/confused when I talk with you. Gonna have to let you go, all but one of you.

If you're famous on the internet it means millions $$$ because of how the internet works. SEO

Keep getting inspired and turn everything else OFF. No energy-sucking distractors for procrastinators.

It's too confusing, gonna have to turn y'all off. Y'all had your chance I'm staying with the best of all.

They try to gain popularity by relaxing lines. Recognize the carnal Christian when you see him--swine!

GIFTS BRING RIFTS

Modern preacher feels forsaken as he wants acceptance and it means false doctrine for the unrepentant.

False doctrine means you can't save 'em cuz they never face their sins followed by repentance.

Let those people in and you'll end up heartbroken, robbed, delayed, mobbed-- it's YOUR HOME, man!

I don't tell you what to think I trigger subconscious analogies IN you and that's recovery: INSIGHT.

SORRY, I HAVE TO LET YOU GO

I'm sorry, I have to let it all go. It's all TOO TOO much and I don't even wanna debate you anymore.

I've done my work, that's all I'm gonna do. The SEO is left to trusted others now--I'm retired/through.

You nickel and dime me to death. Sorry, the business is left to others and what a relief from ridiculous.

Your moral quips aren't worth a thing cuz you relaxed your lines to get the approval of earthlings.

For the sake of our pets, don't let anyone in! Most especially those who don't respect our furry friends.

Time to say goodbye to everything you're known. The Great Division says: Your Time Has Come.

Crossing the Great Divide is this division: If they're not with you 100% then good riddance to em.

This is your last day down with the masses. Now your life will be spectacularly above it all, the joyless.

You've done the work and God is the Rewarder cuz He's not a jerk like those who use you, steal, usurp.

GIFTS BRING RIFTS

I know what this is, if you don't I don't care. It's been defined as a DISCOVERY by those who know more.

My mission is to explode society open with these words--splitting from while resolving all contradictions.

I will not partake in a cat fight with a roundtable of females who feel superior in their lack of knowledge.

JEZEBEL SPIRITS LOVE TO TAKE OVER

It's the Jezebel Spirit in women to take over when they get the chance. Once burned this way, never again!

They "just know" cuz they're (supposedly) leading with their heart but end up hurting all their charges.

They're confused because they're debauched and they're debauched because they're confused.

I shudder when I look back so I've learned I can't: make peace with the past knowing I survived it.

He was my punishment but also my reward since I learned more from that experience than ever before.

How to attain: clear the way, eliminate.

God's timing is everything. Then there won't be anything you can do to stop the inevitable Tsunami.

Every species has its own genotype and genius is ours. Very few realize it, blocked by internal wars.

The Great White Hope has been totally vindicated but that doesn't stop the evil liberals shoving it.

Evil liberals: I'll say it twice. Killing children after birth and you haven't walked away yet? Filthy lice!

GIFTS BRING RIFTS

My husband was sick with cancer with weeks to live but God HEALED him so we'd believe, repent, forgive.

Heartache, betrayal trauma and years of being overlooked/shirked: learn the lesson/God removes curse.

Any woman who puts up with pornography or even views it herself is a slut not protecting the hearth.

WE ALWAYS HAVE THE ADVERSARY

We always have that ol' adversary, honey. Don't think your faith makes life always lovely, it's lonely.

Many Christians left the faith in the 70's to study Hindu deities. I'd hate to be you when you die sweeties.

What Joseph's brothers meant for harm (thought were rid of him) God used for good (they sucked up to him).

We all knew Jussie Smollett was staged just like 99% of all the hate crimes out there--black privilege is here.

They ruin lives with false accusations but it's ok because white people and conservatives don't exist to em.

Crazy liberal feminist causes so much trouble over "climate change" she's thrown off the plane.

Smollett: Not innocent but famous--someone in power called someone else in power and freed his ass.

See them as animals ruled by instinct not men ruled by reason and you'll be rid of resentment/frustrations.

When I wrote at 15 men were like animals in a herd I got a "D" and the secular humanist wasn't pleased.

You meet em then they own you. You wanna be alone and they take it as an insult and attack you.

GIFTS BRING RIFTS

I wanted solitude in a tiny desert (liberal) town–that made me a hater as my world turned upside down.

Liberals can't help but manipulate since they are man-centered and can't allow God to fall into place.

Even the churches attacked me for wanting to be alone. In social generations solitude's a crime, full-blown.

Do you go forward in full faith or draw back due to PTSD from the provocations in the wilderness?

What the enemy meant for harm God is turning around for good FOR THOSE WHO LOVE THE LORD.

GOD USES OVERLOOKED PEOPLE

God uses overlooked people. If they walked you by, God saw who He would use to confront the evil.

Friends: if you felt ignored all your life, like you didn't even exist (disconfirmed) God says "I can use him".

The provocations in my desert wilderness kept me in constant anxiety for decades : that's PTSD.

They kept tearing me down and it was a matter of psychic survival to maintain my identity or drown.

Most sick family systems are only an identity struggle. I saw myself as scholar, sister saw me as criminal.

People who sink to the bottom are what we call "ministry material". They can help because they "know".

The things that happened in a creepy liberal town taught me more than a library of books about the dumbed.

Male writers write various things but females write about themselves and that's always how it's been.

went thru such identity struggles while having no self-defense against invaders I almost didn't make it.

It took decades to learn boundaries. Up till then I was a "good hostess" and let em in, my adversaries.

All they wanted was the pot but I couldn't see that. I've since given it up and thus removed the magnet.

Buying pot before it was legal taught me boundaries the most cuz desperate druggies are pests!

ALCOHOL/DRUGS AND LOWER CHARACTERS

Alcohol also: always involved me with lower characters. It's being clean that establishes borders.

When I finally solved identity struggle I stopped calling myself "Dr." or "Ph.D." but just used my name.

When you're ready to advance (pop on the scene) there's a FRESHNESS to you--this is REVIVAL.

Let your gifts be now stirred up! Let the FIRE in you be rekindled because you finally LOOKED UP!

Your leaves will not whither because you're the spirit of Esther so whatsoever you doeth shall prosper!

Don't let them in or they'll rob you of everything you have. Has it really come down to this? YES!

COMING OUTA YOUR SHELL

It's disgusting what you've been putting up with and I'm deeply ashamed of you creating criminals/sex pots.

Prosper: To break out, to break forth, a break through. This is how nature does it: suddenly it's all you.

GIFTS BRING RIFTS

For success you don't have to convince the world you're great, just ONE person and this union = PAYDAY.

Must KNOW your time has come. This provides the ATOMIC POWER of God's anointing on his children.

Before your time has come = nothing, zilch, zero. After your time has come = everything, thrills, hero.

It WILL BE DONE because God's word will not return void! That's His promise to His loyal girls and boys.

Let me be satisfied with favor and filled with your blessing. Deut. 33: 23. I command your blessing!

You will become an enemy to my enemies for vindication is not mine-- vindication is the Lords!

GOD OVERTURNS FALSE IMAGES OF YOU

God overturns FALSE IMAGE people pegged you with. Let this be overturned right now He declareth.

"Share" is an evil word. Sure we should share but it's tyranny when the top's enriched/the rest murdered.

Don't tell me to share, just go and get your own. Don't you work? I do and thus I'm on the throne.

When they say "share" they're a friggin' communist. Playing Robin Hood with your goods, pissed.

A week of divine turnaround, divine vindication, divine FAVOR! It happens in clumps much like nature.

There's an anointing you carry putting you in the right position but requiring the favor of God for ignition.

God will supernaturally shift things in your family, finances and future opportunities.

GIFTS BRING RIFTS

It's embarrassing looking back so don't do it. You're just seeing the negative not the whole composite.

Pulling back: complaining, doubting, discouragement. When you see these you know you've lost it.

Your self-disgust/beginning to rust or bloat is due to sin. Somehow you've let the devil in/where ya been?

Parent Warnings: Don't let your kids go out with neither boys or girls cuz it's all about sex in this era.

Do NOT leave kids unattended parents for they are having sex! They are primed in the schools, like a hex.

SEX IS ALL THEY THINK ABOUT

Once into sex it's all they think about = NO childhood hobbies, adventures or projects like we had.

Two types: One draws forth with full assurance of faith, the other draws back to provocations in the wilderness.

You will now record and create history by your acts of faith. That's the Esther archetype and it's suddenly.

Parents: Do not EVER allow kids to go into rooms and lock the doors. Not in YOUR house--no more!

Parents: Wise up, this isn't wise sexual expression but kids playing in the toilet and experimenting with smut.

Make sure you're home when they return from school, and don't let their friends come in to locked rooms!

This Tolerance crap has just created sexual perversion and limitless (bottomless pit) evil and sinning.

If you allow their friends to go into locked rooms you're a dam enabler, a frenemy to everyone.

GIFTS BRING RIFTS

You say I'm wrong that they're perverts and promiscuous, taken for granted as normal? Come on now...

They are nothing but creepy pervs--and I'll say it again. Great artists, scientists, elites are rotting with it.

What they do behind closed doors you wouldn't wanna know--they're beneath our contempt ya know.

And these perverts are teaching your kids to do the same? It is truly disgusting and callous the same.

These kids are innocent--straight outa mother's arms. And you're teaching em homo techniques: alarm!

DECOMPENSATION AND COLLAPSED IDENTITY

It's called Decompensation: collapsed identity. The world and self is not what we thought it was, scary.

What held me back in my youth: addictions and arrogance. What works now: let God take care of it.

When I saw her again we resumed where we left off though decades had passed. Wow, life's a gas!

Kids don't have the emotional maturity or background in decency to gain control over sexual anarchy.

It is truly sickening and disgusting what they're teaching your kids and you go along with it? Communists

Communism (top-downism) is accomplished through demoralization: That's how they take control!

If you're a slave to sin God gives you up then you have no hedge against enemies--in flows the crud.

It's just completely and totally disgusting what you've been putting up with in your own homes with kids.

GIFTS BRING RIFTS

I'm telling you don't be a fool! Don't put up with it, out of a fear of being called bigot, intolerant, old fashioned.

A Baptist lady I knew created a convict. A Moron lady I knew justified anything and everything by the twits.

No matter what they could get away with anything. That she called "loving" but rebelled when I disciplined.

When she started putting me down it's like animals in their environment: I went insane by taking it on.

ALL ANIMALS ADAPT TO ENVIRONMENT

Animals all adapt to their environments and confusion brings exhaustion (non-creativity) and sex sin.

The kids aren't allowed to say ANYTHING about ANYTHING but what IS allowed is expressing sexually.

Don't depend on anyone. If she/he's the link, so be it. You don't have to do a thing just relax into it.

It is truly fascinating to understand them. It's all a herd mimicking each other never questioning direction.

Putting on royal apparel: The essential knowing who you are in Christ wrapped in robes of righteousness.

Total purity in righteousness from the finished works of Jesus Christ.

Once you've trudged through sin you know what you're escaping and where you've been/seek salvation.

What I sought thru fruit was cosmic reality but I'm much better of this way: not a diet/dogma but a person.

He is a Rewarder of those faithfully seeking Him--that's what I want!

My pen is in His hands. An emotion or memory arises and He resolves it man.

GIFTS BRING RIFTS

Mentally what's coming up is a lot to handle. Sudden change is imminent and God says just hold on.

Your brothers might not believe in you, your father might not believe in you but God believes in you.

Fresh: not worn or faded, new

My first husband tolerated it, my second husband wouldn't put up with that s**t so I stopped being a twit.

You will not whither. The spirit of Esther is upon you and those leaves never whither.

THE SPIRIT OF ESTHER

The Spirit of Esther: You leaf shall not whither and **WHATEVER** you do shall prosper.

God can make us rich and add no sorrow to it. Anything according to His riches and abundance.

They disrespected my independence so much it was the social that was meaningful to this bunch.

It's scary what people have become and I'd stay alone as much as you can son, now make a ton.

Sin is not just horrible behavior but an empty life.

"Dallas" is one story after another on how family members ruin each other cuz that's life: stormy weather.

They're as dense as they could be having swallowed the one-world narrative: the cosmology of deceit.

We're not all ONE ["we are god"] for we are TWO: saved or damned, righteous or wicked, sinner or repentant.

The false cosmology of ONE-ISM destroys the world as we fail to divide from evil, since it's "all one".

GIFTS BRING RIFTS

ONE-ISM has been a shove-down since kindergarden and it's screwed up our thinking completely.

In the old days when America was decent they saw TWO-ISM: good vs. bad and what to avoid.

With this ONE-IST nightmare people have become like monsters even in their looks: sin makes ya ugly.

If you fail to divide from evil you're gonna prematurely age and look ugly--a muddy aura surrounds ya.

THINKING IT'S ALL GOOD

Thinking it's "all good"--are you kidding me? This shows a seared conscience and an evil destiny.

It's gotten so bad with three generations of ONE-IST crap, now if you stand up for morals they'll ATTACK!

Jesus came to divide--we are to divide from people and the gospel will divide the family--not UNITE.

When the democrats became murderers of little babies already born you became an accomplice, hon'

Women don't know what they're talking about yet repeat the narrative they hear--making em FOOLS not seers.

Wait a minute--the democrats are all for killing live babies after birth. And you're still with this CURSE?

You stupid women you don't know talking about--it's all B.S. outa your mouths! Just shut the fruit up.

Women: Regarding politics you don't know what you're talking about so stop making fools of yourselves.

If you "don't wanna discuss politics" then shut the fruit up, witch! You're just repeating the liberal pitch.

GIFTS BRING RIFTS

ONE-ISM has been a shove-down since kindergarden and it's screwed up our thinking totally hon'

Men were intimidated but are now disgusted with their anti-Trumper wives who are dumb as lice.

Insects, birds and women are all herd animals: they go along with the others no matter how unclever.

Liberal women are so stupid and out of touch they won't even debate--they just 86 you suddenly/walk away.

The less that is happening now the MORE will be happening soon.

LIKE A TSUNAMI

It's like a Tsunami: total quietude just before!   Remember that, always recalling cycles of nature.

Draw em out, throw em off!   Throw em off, draw em out! Stay a mystery or the crazy herd will scoff.

Throw em off--whatever you do get em off your track, their sniffers distracted then back to the pad.

Order PLUS high borders equals DISGUST--remember that. If orderly and reclusive you see the trash.

They think they're great--mentally first rate--yet they are nothing. It's clear, we all know they're bluffing.

Put down anyone you want but when it's President Trump, you're on my s***list and I'm really pist.

You put down President Trump and I dis-friend you so fast and block ya too. Silly dumb broads, pooh.

The Women for Trump are gorgeous and brilliant specimens of the female gender unlike you bartender.

GIFTS BRING RIFTS

You disgusting liberal democrat women--of all people, you are for killing live born babies? VERMIN!

You would've preferred a criminal married to a rapist who woulda let all of Africa/Mexico in our midst.

Rather than spreading a lie while knowing nothing--which you admit eventually--please stop babbling.

Women: If all their friends suddenly became pro-Trump they'd go that way. Herd animals, unthinking.

IT'S THE STYLE TO HATE TRUMP

It's the style, the fashion, to hate Trump. Is that the extent of your ability to think and discern you chump?

Don't worry they don't see your mistakes yet cuz on the net there's no reason to focus on you twit.

When Barry's in GITMO everyone like this will go down with him including his partner in crime Michael.

They try to make you "face reality" by showing you repulsive/horrible things. Stay HIGH and say "bye bye".

For you gotta get your mind outa the gutter if you want to be catapulted to the greatest/seen as so clever.

I can't get walled in enough

I've given you all this, you don't need me now.

What you mentioned must have been my delirium in my desert wilderness stage of facing self and sin.

Yes it was horrible how they treated ____ but that's the dynamics of the mob whether family or group.

Trump's Rally is monumental history. Revitalization Movements occur with charismatic leaders recurrently.

GIFTS BRING RIFTS

Women: Mimicking the narrative but never questioning it. If you give em facts they'll escape/call you s**t.

Women: You make such asses of yourselves mimicking the narrative and never questioning it--just shut up!

PASSWORD TO GOD'S BLESSINGS: THANKS!

But then you realize the password is gratitude: just yesterday I recalled all He gave me and was moved.

You realize: so what if it hasn't happened yet? The project is segmented--you finished this, now that.

So "it" didn't happen today--again this is only a small part and your impatience is showing again, ok?

How else can God test your faith than to not give you what you want then watch what happens to the grunt?

Continue to wait while you thank Him for all He has done. That's what wins his attention and rewards hon'

Continue to wait happily. Stay cheerful while in service while anticipating the reward from Big Daddy.

Continue to wait while thanking Him for all He has done: that's what gets his attention/wins his reward son.

Why just yesterday I was thankful for God putting me in this place. Then today anger/it was all erased.

Knowing you must wait--like a farmer waiting for harvest--frees you from pain. Plant seed, do your thing.

During the wait stay properly nourished/rest or you'll get down/lose faith in self or that God's the best.

I know I have to wait and that I'll be tested as I wait cuz the wait is the whole test for the first-rate.

GIFTS BRING RIFTS

Impatience is the boomer's major defect. They want it all now, very entitled, and so it is with the Elect.

Let God fill in the steps! It isn't just you but it is on your behalf, for your benefit: God is Rewarder--it's legit.

You don't know all that must happen--the bigger it is! Your destiny is giant, cuz God designed this.

Your destiny may be much bigger than you know, cuz it's predestined by the Almighty Head Honcho.

LET GOD FILL IN THE STEPS

So let God fill in the steps while you relax! Just believe it'll happen because you know He paid the price.

Remember: Waiting is the whole thing and you're doing it now--a beginning, middle, end then it's over.

My Lord no one could've ever done this had it not been God. You were a co-Creator with Him: be awed!

Don't get impatient but think: maybe it's the middle of the wait then the end will come--see it that way.

God put great ideas in you and has the link prepared too. It's a giant puzzle with the end coming soon.

You will be remunerated for work/back payments too. God pays double for your trouble with fools.

If I think it's the beginning or middle of the wait I know to just kick back for a month, relax, everything's ok.

Knowing it's how God does things--plant, wait, harvest--is so immensely and wonderfully relieving.

Just get high, sweeten/streamline your environment, plan your wardrobe for the public, be thankful amen.

GIFTS BRING RIFTS

There is an end to the wait, just know that. You're in the middle and it's just not Your Season yet.

When your season (your Day) comes it'll be like a Tsunami. Know that and just prepare for harvest honey.

The problem is not how to get to success but how to handle it when you get there. Wise saying

While waiting: why not relax, watch old movies, do whatever you want to improve yourself.

Ok if I have to wait on the Lord I will happily wait on the Lord. If that's His main thing, I will joyfully do it.

It's not that they were deliberately imposing on you but just desperately wanted what you had--forget it.

I'M GONNA ENJOY WAITING FOR GOD

I'm gonna enjoy waiting because I know that's what God wants me to do. Building faith is ok too.

Prosper: To break out, to break forth, a break through. This is how nature does it: suddenly it's all you.

I've let go of all human crutches now. At first it was scary but then relieving to just rely upon Father, God.

It was terrifying as human crutches went away, then I opened up to a new vista and light of a new day.

WAITING is the new obstruction but actually it doesn't have to be. See it as a crucial phase and relax, see?

You did your work now it's maturing underground. It's not seen yet but when it bursts open, you're renowned.

The more you hear nothing the more you're gonna hear everything: Know that's how it works, earthling.

GIFTS BRING RIFTS

I know I'm doing God's work and that He sticketh closer than a brother. He's here now: silent Thunder.

Your season: explosion! One minute before your season: nothing! Remember that and get ready.

It's when things are most quiet, ineffectual, looks like nothings' ever gonna happen, then EXPLOSION.

Before Tsunami the waves go way out: silence, waterless, quiet--then the wave comes in (they all buy it).

You're a success whether "they" like it or not. Be a success before success then be ready for God.

REAL SUCCESS IS A TIDAL WAVE

Real success resembles Tsunami: A giant wave of frenetic activity just after nothing, zero, silence, apathy.

I'll write all about waiting while I wait. Since this is the main thing I see how clever you are, the Great.

Kick back, watch old movies. Plan a future of abundance, look out the window, do anything but worry.

Everything at once, then nothing. Nothing, then everything at once: that's life's cycles on this ball of mud.

Don't obstruct God's underground work with your impatience or petty strivings to make it happen, relax!

Not a drop or a trickle--that's a sign of Tsunami coming, opposite to little. For this reprieve be thankful.

Not a trickle? Hurray! That means in just a little bit it'll be a tidal wave.

Seasons are the UNFORCED cycles of nature. That means you just gotta wait and turn inward: mature.

GIFTS BRING RIFTS

In other words, all of life is ebb and flow. That's all you gotta know: just WAIT for the sudden growth.

Not even a trickle I feel so grateful cuz I know what it means: silence precedes an explosion, monumental.

Someone will see it. You'll be discovered so it's good you made it all available but now just wait for it.

FOOD AND CHEMICAL OBSTRUCTIONS

After eating a bear claw, a danish and an eclair she was so sick from chemicals she was dumbed/lost flair.

Read labels on Wallmart Bakery goods: It doesn't say flour, dairy & fruit but lots of chemicals/poisons too.

Immune system read "bakery" as a terrible poison and shot antigens at it all night: acute pain/spiritual blight.

If it's just one meal it's about Satiety Power so you can go without food longer, like bread and butter.

Man has been mixing foods in one meal for thousands years but now we must separate foods outa fear.

Get a breadmaker and make it all from raisin-breads to fruitcakes and things from the best ingredients.

Everything has SOY in it--get a bread-maker to not be a slave or victim of it. The best grains--and store it.

Monasteries had a bakery, a dairy and in the summer fruit trees making tasty butter/bread/jam for thee.

My handsome sleek dad practically lived on bread and butter and he was known as Mr. Dapper.

The bread is just a delivery system for the delicious and absolutely necessary animal fat digested slowly.

GIFTS BRING RIFTS

Animal fat in the form of butter made him quick, energetic and alert--a real go-getter after creamy dessert.

My Scottish ancestors collapsed calories that way--baked bread and LOTSA butter then fasted all day.

My handsome dad always put a half inch butter on a cracker--that was dinner and he woke up thinner.

BREAD, BUTTER AND FRUIT ONCE ONLY

Bread and butter then I put my mind on other matters meanwhile the kitchen stays free of clutter.

The Land of Milk and Honey also had Bread. That's all they ate in those days and they were well-fed.

Something soft, warm, filling and sweet in the morning. Hasn't it always been that way--so comforting?

Then in the afternoon just a piece of fruit, a nut or nothing. Forget vegetables they have anti-nutrients.

Went back to salsa & guacamole--it didn't work. Things keep changing and we re-adapt or it's the hearse.

You wouldn't give the (carnivore) lion a cantaloupe so please don't give your cats vegan food you dope.

Escaped California to new home in middle America. Crickets at night, crows at dawn, cows walk by ya.

The chemically sensitive (MCS) are often ex-heroine addicts, alcoholics or failed suicide attempts.

I'm a vegetarian now, I do fruit and dairy. I have hips now but who wants to look like a stick I guess.

I had no power as vegan sticking to fruit and veggies. I can eat and go all day now or 36 hours happily.

GIFTS BRING RIFTS

That was a miserable trip being a vegan and having to eat all that. Six times a day but I'm just one--max.

I now the cows, they're well cared for and happy. They must be milked and I'm now extremely healthy.

RAW MILK MACHINES

Raw milk is sold across Europe in machines. But not here, most so-called heath experts see it as obscene.

Geniuses live on cheese and crackers cuz they don't have time to fix a meal. Really it's all you need.

My berry yogurt milkshakes with nutbutter in em. For breakfast it's a lactofruitarian gem friends.

Then later what the heck have some garlic bread soaked in butter then later go alkaline (fruit) to sleep better.

Chicken Caesars for husband but I'm not into meat. I think dairy will make my daily diet non-deficient.

TODAY: Shrimp Louie for hubby but Greek Salad for me.

KAREN KELLOCK PH.D.

M.S. Political Science, San Diego State. Ph.D. in Psychology, University of California Irvine. Postdoctoral: UCI School of Medicine, Dept. of Psychiatry [NIMH Grants]. Developed the Debris Theory of Disease, a theory of system pathology in 120 books and 22 textbooks for the general public. The theory has a general formula: All disease is obstruction, all recovery is elimination, all success is attraction. The three obstructions are people, habit and food. Remove obstruction and snap to your goals, waiting in the wings.